CASTAWAY ON CAPE BRETON:

Ensign Prenties' *Narrative*, 1780

&

Samuel Burrows' *Narrative* of Shipwreck on the Cheticamp Coast, 1823

CASTAWAY
ON Cape Breton

Ensign Prenties' *Narrative*, 1780
Edited with an Historical Setting and Notes
by G. G. Campbell

TO WHICH IS ADDED

Samuel Burrows' *Narrative*
of Shipwreck
on the Cheticamp Coast, 1823
With Notes on Acadians Who Cared for the Survivors
by Charles D. Roach

Breton Books
Wreck Cove, Cape Breton Island
1991

CASTAWAY ON CAPE BRETON

COMPILATION © Breton Books, 1991

Canadian Cataloguing in Publication Data
Prenties, S. W. (Samuel Waller).
    Castaway on Cape Breton
    Includes bibliographical references.
    ISBN 1-895415-00-4

1. Prenties, S. W. (Samuel Waller). 2. Burrows,
Samuel. 3. St. Lawrence (Ship). 4. Wyton (Ship).
5. Shipwrecks — Nova Scotia — Cape Breton Island —
History. 6. Survival after airplane accidents,
shipwrecks, etc. I. Campbell, G. G. (George
Graham), 1904-1972. II. Burrows, Samuel.

G530.P8 1991   910. 4'5   C92-007110-4

The cover illustration of Ensign Prenties at Margaree
Harbour is from Robert Pollard's 1784 engraving of
"The Departure," a painting by Robert Smirke. A print
of "The Departure" is in the James McConnell Library in
Sydney, Nova Scotia, part of the Cape Breton Regional
Library Collection. See note 32, page 117.

TABLE OF CONTENTS

CASTAWAY ON CAPE BRETON

Introduction to the 1991 Edition

Castaway on Cape Breton brings together Cape Breton Island's two most harrowing narratives of shipwreck. These are the words of survivors. Ensign Prenties' *Narrative* is more widely known, having seen several printings since 1780. But Samuel Burrows' account was nearly lost. This 1823 disaster is not included in the standard lists of North American shipwreck narratives, and we know of only two extant copies of the original book. Although a version appeared in 1980 in *Cape Breton's Magazine*—this is the first appearance of the entire book in 165 years.

Prenties' account of his wreck and journey around northern Cape Breton survived because it played an obvious role in history. He carried papers that had implications in the conquest of North America. On the other hand, Samuel Burrows' *Narrative* is the story of a person of no particular rank or fame, engaged in very ordinary work—a seaman on a trading vessel, now writing of the shipwreck to earn money for his support, no longer able to sail. He had survived his fourth wreck. It is fair to assume he would have sailed again, had he had legs. And while it in no way detracts from the excruciating suffering of Prenties and his companions, Prenties is writing for history. He is writing to a specific military ear, reporting on his mission, hoping to further his career. Samuel Burrows is writing to the rest of us, hoping, as his first publisher wrote, to earn a little money. We eavesdrop on Prenties; Burrows speaks to us directly. Prenties fills out our picture of history. Burrows indelibly marks our lives.

The original *Castaway on Cape Breton* included only the Ensign Prenties *Narrative* and G. G. Campbell's Prologue, Epilogue, and extensive Notes. In his Introduction, editor Campbell wrote that he tried to place Prenties' "misadventure in its historical setting, and to record what can be gleaned about Prenties himself.... I found it advisable to change the paragraphing and eliminate many commas, for Prenties uses commas in ways to hamper the modern reader." We have regularized Samuel Burrows' paragraphs as well.

We have incorporated many of Dr. Campbell's footnotes into the body of the text. His longer notes will be found at the end of the book. As a careful local historian, he uses the notes "chiefly as a repository of little-known or forgotten facts about the places visited by Prenties in his woeful peregrination round and through Cape Breton. I have done so with diffidence, for notes are the bane of the busy reader; but with confidence also that there are those who live in the island and some, perhaps, dwelling in exile who cherish

the land and its past, even in those inaccessible, untrodden paths
that so few people see.

"And Prenties, though he did not visit the island under ideal conditions, did contrive to get into outlandish places. Even the parts
now inhabited were desolate wilderness. Apart from a solitary
army post on Sydney Harbour, a handful of people in ruined
Louisbourg and the infrequent Acadian hamlet near St. Peters and
on Isle Madame, only the occasional band of Indians occupied the
island. Scotland had not yet arrived, and the Loyalists had still to
find a destination."

To Dr. Campbell's edition, we have added the entire text of Samuel Burrows' 1823 account of the shipwreck of the *Wyton* on the
west coast of northern Cape Breton, somewhere near present-day
Fishing Cove—along the same coast Prenties travelled in 1780. In
1823, the coastline was still not populated north of Cheticamp.
Cape Breton Island had only recently been re-annexed to Nova
Scotia and land was opening for settlement—but non-development
had been the Cape Breton government's conspicuous achievement
during forty years as a province. Acadians had lived in the Cheticamp region since at least the 1790's—but north of that was a
harbourless, empty coastline. No settlers came to Pleasant Bay until around 1828.

Dr. Campbell thanked two people for their help: Dr. William
Mould, Head of the English Department at Sydney Academy, who
had read his manuscript and proved "a strict warden of the language," and "Mary Fraser of the James McConnell Memorial Library, for I have made extravagant demands on her patience and
expert knowledge." This new, enlarged edition of *Castaway on
Cape Breton* is deeply indebted to Ms. Fraser as well. She first told
us of the existence of Samuel Burrows' extraordinary *Narrative.*

Dr. Campbell dedicated his edition to his grandchildren: Marion,
Jennifer, Jill, Gordon, George-Angus and Robert.

We want to dedicate this book
to the 150th Anniversary of Sydney Academy
and to the memory of Dr. G. G. Campbell
Principal of Sydney Academy
from 1935 to 1968.

Ronald Caplan
Bonnie Thompson
Wreck Cove
1991

Ensign Prenties' *Narrative*

OF A

SHIPWRECK

ON THE

ISLAND OF CAPE BRETON

IN A VOYAGE FROM QUEBEC

1780

PROLOGUE TO PRENTIES' *NARRATIVE*
by G. G. Campbell

IN THE AUTUMN OF 1775 Canada was threatened by two invading armies. One of these had been on the move since May, when Ethan Allen and his Green Mountain boys surprised and seized Fort Ticonderoga. From Ticonderoga, the ninety-mile length of Lake Champlain pointed the way to Canada; but it was some weeks before Congress, hesitant in its course, resolved by force of arms to bring the colony on the St. Lawrence into the fold of the Revolution. Thereafter the expedition gathered strength and momentum, cleared Lake Champlain of British shipping and took, one after the other, the forts at Crown Point, Chambly and St. Jean. By mid-November this army, commanded by General Richard Montgomery, had occupied Montreal.

In the meantime, a force of some eight hundred men under Benedict Arnold was making its way from Massachusetts up the Kennebec River, and down the Chaudière to the St. Lawrence. No fortified posts disputed its passage, but a difficult terrain, wintry weather and a dearth of supplies made the journey an arduous and memorable achievement. This army ended its march opposite Quebec about a week before Montgomery occupied Montreal.

Canada was in no way to withstand these invasions, inconsiderable though they were. Just a year before, mounting unrest and disorder in New England had prompted Sir Guy Carleton, Governor and Commander-in-Chief in Canada, to send most of his regular troops to Boston. As a result, when the affair at Lexington and the blood bath at Bunker Hill turned unrest into open rebellion, fewer than a thousand trained soldiers stood guard in Canada. The number dwindled as, one by one, the forts on the Champlain waterway fell to Montgomery's Americans. And when Governor Carleton was forced from Montreal he escaped with not so much as a corporal's guard, leaving the garrison behind as prisoners. When the little vessel in which he got away neared Quebec, Carleton could see the army of Benedict Arnold already in position to besiege the city. He knew that Montgomery, victorious in Montreal, would soon march to join with Arnold—and Canada was almost bare of defenders.

Quebec, grey old city, huddled behind walls on Cape Diamond. Her guns outmatched the artillery the Americans had brought with them, but the walls themselves were manned for the most part by poorly trained militiamen. Timely help arrived when a man called Allan MacLean led into the city a body of men he had recruited in what is now Upper New York State. Known as the Royal Highland Emigrants, they were the nucleus of what was soon to be the 84th Regiment of Foot. Carleton's arrival, after his narrow escape in Montreal, gave spirit and direction to defence preparations. Old soldiers put on their uniforms, disaffected persons were expelled from the city, while young recruits went to train in the citadel. So when Montgomery brought his army down river to join Arnold's, the old city on the rock was ready at least for a fight.

Montgomery chose the early morning of New Year's Eve for a two-pronged attack on the lower town. The fighting took place in darkness, wind and blizzard. When it was over Quebec stood bloodied but secure within her walls, while enemy dead littered the streets of the lower town. In the aftermath, a hand protruding from a snowdrift led searchers to a frozen corpse. They carried it into the upper town where a woman called Elizabeth Prenties looked on the icy countenance and identified the dead man as General Montgomery.

Elizabeth was the wife of Miles Prenties, one-time provost marshal in Wolfe's army, of late years innkeeper in Quebec's upper town. Long before, Miles Prenties and Richard Montgomery had fought together at the siege of Louisbourg. Then they both, and Guy Carleton as well, had served in the two campaigns that brought General Wolfe to the Plains of Abraham, and finally gave Canada to the British crown. In the years of peace after the war Montgomery sometimes visited in Quebec, where he stayed at Prenties' Tavern. Now, by war's strange fortunes, the three old comrades were met again at Quebec, with Montgomery an enemy and rebel. Carleton saw to it that the dead general got a military funeral, and himself supplied a coffin. Rebel he was, beyond all doubt; but first he was friend and comrade-in-arms, and a fellow Irishman. Prenties, too, hailed from Ireland.

After Montgomery's abortive attack, the enemy made no further attempt to storm the city. And when spring swept the St. Lawrence free of ice, reinforcements came up river to lift the siege. The Americans went off in swift, disordered retreat, with Carleton hard on their heels, and by midsummer all Canada was free. Although not notable as a feat of arms, Quebec's stubborn resistance did at least convince Congress that Canada was not to be easily swallowed up in the Revolution. And imperial ministers in London could read the lesson that, from the far end of Lake Superior down to the Gulf, Quebec was Britain's one strong bastion, her one hope of saving Canada from the wreckage of empire. For years to come the old city was to be the depot into which poured the men and supplies that were to sustain and hold a few meagre strongholds lost in the distances of the west.

INEVITABLY THE WAR BROUGHT a measure of prosperity to Quebec. As proprietor of one of the city's two hostels, Miles Prenties found it expedient to move his business to larger quarters. His new building, a large stone house on rue Buade, already had a certain notoriety. Carved in stone over its entrance was an enigmatic device that invariably attracted attention. It consisted of the gilded image of a dog chewing on the thigh bone of a man, and the following inscription:

> Je suis un chien qui ronge l'os
> En le rongeant je prends mon repos.
> Un temps viendra qui n'est pas venu
> Que je morderai celui m'aura mordu.[1]

> (I am a dog, on a bone I gnaw
> Biding my time I gnaw and gnaw.
> The time is not yet but soon will be
> When I will bite who has bitten me.)

A nineteenth-century novelist would one day make famous this House of the Golden Dog.[2] But in Prenties' time it was known simply as Prenties' Tavern—*Taverne de Prenties.* Within its walls Elizabeth Prenties presided over a busy establishment, with four negro slaves, two indentured servants and hired help as well, all to be kept to their duties.

The Prenticses had three children, a daughter[3] and two sons. With the coming of war, the three men of the family were taken up with military duties. Miles himself went back into uniform as soon as Quebec got word of the American invasions; he was assigned again to the post of provost marshal, this time with the rank of captain. His two sons, Samuel Walter and John Thomas, the one just over twenty, the other in his late teens, had their baptism of fire in the confused street fighting of New Year's Eve. Walter served with the Royal Highland Emigrants in that

1. Notes and Sources begin on page 107.

affair and in the pursuit that sent the Americans homeward after the lifting of the siege. Then, as the war dragged out its length and the colony settled down to wartime ways, young Walter spent the fighting seasons in different outposts and retired to winter quarters in the House of the Golden Dog. Most of his postings away from Quebec he spent on the Champlain waterway.

For more than a century this celebrated ribbon of water had cut across the undefined and fluctuating boundary separating the colonies of England from those of France. Armies drilled in European warfare had manoeuvered and clashed along its length, while Indian war parties used it in bloody raids on frontier settlements. The British conquest of Canada had put an end to such activities; for fifteen years subjects of the king moved freely and safely between Albany on the Hudson and Sorel on the St. Lawrence. But when England and her colonies went to war, the waterway again became an avenue where men moved furtively and on guard. Spies and rival scouting parties went out stealthily, mixed war parties of Indians and whites pushed their canoes north or south to spread havoc and terror, while forlorn companies of dispossessed Loyalists made their cautious way towards asylum and exile in Canada. Along the waterway had come Montgomery's invading army; another might well follow the same route. On the other hand, strategists in London and Quebec were planning to use it to take an army into the heartland of the rebellious colonies. So once again the old forts at Chambly, St. Jean, Crown Point and Ticonderoga stood frowning guard on either side of a disputed frontier.

IT WAS MIDSUMMER OF 1777 before the British could counter Montgomery's invasion with one of their own. More than a year in preparation, the expedition finally mustered at St. Jean. General John Burgoyne crossed the Atlantic with an army of seven thousand men, and in due course a veritable armada moved south along Lake Champlain. With it, in their long canoes, went five hundred Indian warriors, led by the celebrated partisan, St. Luc de La Corne.

As Burgoyne moved deeper and deeper into rebel territory, word came back to St. Jean that he had occupied Ticonderoga and was moving on to the Hudson. In late August came the disconcerting spectacle of Indian warriors pushing their canoes out of the south towards St. Jean. Some found it ominous that Burgoyne's Indian allies were deserting him, but he seemed to be in no serious trouble. Late in September there was news of heavy fighting at Stillwater on the Hudson; and then the devastating and incredible tidings that Gentleman Johnny and his splendid army, to the last man and the last gun, were captives of the American rebels.

The onset of winter gave Canada a breathing spell in which to recover from the shock of Burgoyne's disaster. But in the early summer of 1778, when Sir Frederick Haldimand arrived in Quebec to replace Sir Guy Carleton, the prospect from the Château St. Louis could hardly have been more threatening, more devoid of hope. A thousand miles away in the western wilderness stood the fortified settlement of Michilimackinac. Between it and Montreal, military establishments at Detroit, Niagara, Oswego and Carleton Island were charged with preventing the Americans from getting a footing on the Great Lakes. On these feeble posts, and on the forts guarding the Champlain waterway, the integrity of Canada depended. To man these scattered posts, and to supply them over vast distances with the materials of sustenance and war, was for five years to come Haldimand's first charge.

His position was extraordinarily difficult, his burden of responsibility very heavy. The people he governed were by no means wholly reconciled to British rule. And it must have been clear to the lonely man in the Château St. Louis that whether England was left with any part of her North American dominion depended above all on the attitude of the Canadians; if they joined the Revolution, there would no longer be a British Canada. All the governor's tact, firmness and vigilance were exercised to keep his people in active loyalty or, failing that, in passive acceptance of British rule. To add to his burdens came the Loyalists, hundreds of them, homeless, propertyless, peremptory in demanding assistance from the king on whose behalf they had lost everything.

When winter closed the St. Lawrence, Haldimand was marooned. Five hundred miles to the south Sir Henry Clinton, with a large British army, held the port and city of New York. But the American armies hemmed him in and controlled most of the country between New York and the St. Lawrence, cutting off all effective communication by land. In the open months of the year dispatches between Quebec and New York went by way of the St. Lawrence, then down the Atlantic coast, although the gulf swarmed with American privateers on the look-out for British shipping. In winter couriers went on foot by way of Lake Temiscouata and the St. John River to Halifax, thence to New York by sea. In fact, communication with New York was so difficult, so uncertain, that Haldimand once passed nine months without word from Sir Henry Clinton.

LATE IN 1780, when the St. Lawrence was beginning to choke with ice, Haldimand sent off a bundle of dispatches with Ensign Drummond of the 44th Regiment, who was going to New York to take up a commission in the 17th Dragoons. He gave duplicates of the dispatches to Ensign Walter Prenties, also bound for New York but on a different vessel. By yet a third ship, Haldimand sent word to Clinton that dispatches were on the way. Then, as the river closed, he took up his long winter vigil on Cape Diamond.

Ensign Walter Prenties was off on a notable adventure. And it may have been with a measure of relief that Haldimand and his headquarters staff saw the young man disappear down the reaches of the river. The truth is Ensign Prenties was an importunate youth, fertile of grievances, a law to himself, disdainful of military protocol. Failing to get his way with his immediate superiors, he had the disconcerting habit of by-passing the chain of command to appeal directly to the Commander-in-Chief, a habit that did not endear him to senior officers. And even in a time when the purchase of an army commission was held to allow much freedom of action to the purchaser, Prenties presumed too much.

He had bought his commission in the 84th Regiment in July, 1778.[4] Thereafter he spent little time with his unit, detachments of which were posted to places far distant from Quebec. On the plea of ill-health, Prenties contrived to remain in the city on continuing leave. Unwell he may have been, but he managed to hold a job in the commissariat, even while demanding his pay as an ensign in the 84th. Ultimately it took a peremptory order from Haldimand himself to get him back to duty with his regiment.

But not for long. Early in 1780 Prenties appealed to Haldimand, again on the grounds of ill-health, for six months' leave. Continued service in Canada, he said, would certainly cause his death, to avert which he wished to try a European climate. He could not in duty, he insisted, "wait patiently his decaying and annihilation in this country, in which state he must be totally useless to the service."[5] Since his appeal was accompanied by a doctor's certificate, Haldimand chose to send him to New York with the dispatches. In a letter of introduction addressed to General Clinton he stated that Prenties had been granted permission "to winter in a southern climate."

After his Cape Breton experience and a visit to England, Prenties was to return to duty with his regiment. His relations with regimental officers were to become more and more exacerbated, until he was almost continually under arrest. But never again is there mention of his health as contributing to his difficulties. It is tempting to assume that his sojourn in Cape Breton brought about an improvement in health, but this hardly seems probably. Details of that sojourn are abundantly set forth in Prenties' *Narrative*.

END of the PROLOGUE to Ensign Prenties' *Narrative*

Advertisement by S. W. Prenties

If a genuine and authentic narrative of events which may be justly reckoned extraordinary, though they come not up to the standard of adventures, be thought equally interesting with a fictitious Novel, or an improbable Romance, no apology will be required for the present publication. Indeed, to apologize for so innocent and even laudable an attempt as that to entertain the Public, by any species of composition, satisfied as it is by custom, should always be thought superfluous; and though that end should not be attained by the following narration, yet at least it may be interesting to professional men, who are continually exposed to the same disasters. Like the draughts of rocks and quicksands in their charts, it may serve to direct them how to avoid the danger, or, when once involved in it, how to conduct themselves through it.

In the relating of our transactions at sea, all technical terms have been avoided as far as possible; yet on some occasions they could not be wholly dispensed with. The frequent use of egotism will be excused by those who consider its necessity, from the nature of the subject.

Though in narratives of this kind there are sometimes considerable embellishments and exaggerations, yet the authenticity of the facts here related, cannot so reasonably be called in question, as those of an anonymous production: for it will not appear probable to any thinking person, that I should put my name to a relation either exceeding or short of the truth, when it is considered, that there are several persons living, who would be ready to contradict my assertions.

Ensign Prenties' *Narrative*

ON THE 17TH OF NOVEMBER 1780, I embarked on
board the St. Lawrence brigantine, then lying in the basin
of Quebec and bound to New York, being charged with
dispatches from General Haldimand, commander in chief
in that province, to Sir Henry Clinton. The same day, on
receiving our sailing orders, we weighed anchor and
dropped down to the harbour called Patrick's Hole, in the
island of Orleans, in company with a schooner bound to
the same port, on board of which was an Ensign Drummond of the 44th regiment, with duplicates of General
Haldimand's dispatches. In this place we were detained
six days by a contrary wind; at the expiration of which
time the frost had set in with prodigious severity, and the
ice was forming fast in all parts of the river. Had the wind
continued unfair for a few days longer, we should have
been entirely blocked up by it, and had happily escaped
the calamities which afterwards befell us.

On the 24th, the wind being fair, we got under weigh and proceeded down the river St. Lawrence as far as the Brandy Pots, islands so called, about forty leagues from Quebec. At this place the wind veered about to the northeast, which obliged us again to anchor. The weather continued intensely cold; and the vessel, being leaky, made so much water as to render it necessary to keep one pump continually going. A change of wind soon after enabled us to proceed on our voyage and to make the island of Anticosti, which is at the mouth of the river St. Lawrence; when the wind coming round again to the eastward, we were obliged to beat off and on between this island and Cape Roziere for four days; our vessel at the same time increasing her leaks to such a degree that we were under the necessity of rigging the other pump, and of keeping them both constantly at work.

Being now in a higher latitude, the severity of the cold had increased in proportion, and the ice began to form so fast about the ship as to alarm us exceedingly, lest we should be entirely surrounded by it, which we only prevented by cutting and breaking vast quantities from her sides. To this task, with that of keeping the pumps at work, the crew together with the passengers were scarcely equal, only nineteen persons being on board, of whom six were passengers and the remainder very indifferent seamen. As for the master, from whom in the present emergency we might have expected some degree of exertion, instead of attending to his duty and the preservation of his ship, he remained continually in a state of intoxication in his cabin.

On the 29th the wind came round to the north-west, and we proceeded down the gulf of St. Lawrence with two feet water in the ship's hold. The wind kept gradually increasing till the 1st of December, when it blew a perfect gale from the north-west quarter; and the ship's crew being now almost overcome with cold and fatigue, seeing no prospect of gaining upon the leak, the water having already increased to four feet in the hold, nor a possibility of making any port, they came to the resolution of working no longer at the pumps; which was unanimously agreed to by all the foremast men. They accordingly left off working and declared themselves quite indifferent about their fate, preferring the alternative of going to the bottom together with the vessel to that of suffering such severe and incessant labour in so desperate a situation.

Their fatigues, it must be confessed, from the 17th of November had been excessive; and though hope might still remain, yet our present circumstances were such as to exclude all probability at least of saving the vessel. However, by the force of persuasion and promises, together with the timely distribution of a pint of wine per man, which I had fortunately brought on board, they were diverted from this desperate resolution, but with great reluctance, saying with some truth, as we afterwards experienced, and with more than they themselves were aware of, that whether the vessel filled or not was a matter of no consequence. This delay, though not exceeding a quarter of an hour, had increased the depth of water another foot; but the men added to their exertions, being encouraged by the wine which was issued to them every half-hour, [and] succeeded so far as to reduce the water in the space of two hours to less than three feet. The captain still remained in his cabin.

During the 2nd and 3rd of December the gale seemed to increase rather than to diminish. The ice formed so thick on the ship's sides as to impede her way very much through the water; which furnished us with a new labour, that of cutting it off as fast as it formed, with saws and axes. The leak continued to gain ground. The schooner that was in company, far from being able to afford us any assistance, was in as leaky a condition as our own vessel, having struck upon some rocks at the island of Coudres through the ignorance or neglect of her pilot. A heavy snow beginning to fall, it was with the utmost difficulty we could get sight of each other, though at no great distance, and in order not to part company, [we] fired a gun every half-hour. The schooner at length made no answer to our guns, whence we concluded she had foundered; nor were we wrong in our supposition. There were sixteen persons on board, every one of whom perished. (*The vessel carrying Ensign Drummond was driven ashore on Anticosti with the loss of all on board.*)

On the following day the gale increased prodigiously and the sea began to run high, with a heavy fall of snow, so as to prevent our seeing twenty yards ahead of the vessel. The men being excessively fatigued, the water had risen to its usual quantity of between four and five feet. The mate, whom I have not yet taken notice of, an intelligent young man and well acquainted with his profession, judged from the distance we had run that we could not now be far from the Magdalen Islands, which lie about midway in the Gulf of St. Lawrence.

These islands are nothing more than a cluster of rocks, some appearing above and others hidden under the water, and have been fatal to many vessels. Seamen wish often to make them in fine weather, as they serve to take a new departure from; but in foggy or blowing weather they as studiously avoid them. The mate's conjecture was but too well founded; for in less than two hours we heard the sea breaking upon the rocks, and soon after discovered the principal island, called the Deadman, close under our lee, the point of which it was with the greatest difficulty that we weathered. Having happily cleared the main island, we were still far from thinking ourselves secure; for being unable on account of the heavy fall of snow to see many yards ahead of the vessel, and being in the midst of the small islands, there appeared very little probability that we should pass clear of them all in the same manner. Not being able to distinguish any one in time to avoid it, we were obliged to leave the vessel to the direction of Providence, and fortunately, I might say almost miraculously, ran through them all without damage.

The anxiety and perturbation of mind that the crew and passengers were in, while in the midst of these rocks, may be easily conceived: and now that the danger was over, it turned out to be a fortunate occurrence for us; for by this time, the sailors being ready to sink under the accumulated distresses of cold and fatigue, and depressed by the little hopes they had of saving the vessel, had nearly determined a second time to quit the pumps and leave the vessel to her fate, when acquiring fresh spirits from the danger we had escaped, and, as the vulgar are generally inclined to superstition, attributing what was perhaps accident alone to the immediate interposition of Providence, they agreed to continue their efforts a little longer; towards which they were likewise not a little encouraged by the wine which I distributed to them occasionally.

During the night the gale continuing, and the sea running very high, we were apprehensive of being what seamen call pooped, or having the stern or poop of the vessel beaten in by the waves; which happened in fact as we apprehended: for about five in the morning of the 5th, a large wave broke on the ship's quarter, which stove in our dead lights, filled the cabin, and washed the master out of his bed, where he had remained ever since the commencement of the gale.

The accident was attended with worse consequences than we at first imagined; for we soon discovered from the increase of the leaks that the stern-post had been parted by the impulse of the sea. Having nothing in the after-hold, no other resource was left but that of attempting to stop the leaks with beef, which we cut into small pieces for that purpose: but this expedient we soon found ineffectual, and the water continued to gain on us faster than ever. The sailors finding all their labour fruitless, and the leak, which was constantly increasing before, now rendered by our late misfortune entirely irreparable, abandoned themselves totally to despair and again refused to work at the pumps any longer. They had not however long remained inactive before we contrived once more to persuade them to make another effort to clear the vessel; when, to our great surprise and consternation, we found the pumps so hard frozen that it was impossible to move them.

All endeavours now to keep the ship clear were ineffectual, so that in a very short time she filled to the water's edge. Having no longer, as we imagined, the smallest foundation for hope, we resigned ourselves with as much fortitude as possible to our fate, which we expected every moment to be that of going to the bottom. Notwithstanding, when the vessel was quite full, we observed she was very little deeper in the water than before; and then recollecting a circumstance which the trouble and confusion we had been in had almost obliterated, namely, that we had a quantity of lumber on board, we immediately accounted for the phenomenon of her not sinking beyond a certain depth in the water, and began to recall hopes of saving our lives at least, if we could but prevent her from oversetting till we could make the island of St. John's (*now Prince Edward Island*), or some other island in the gulf.

Having no guns on deck, and not much lumber to render the ship top-heavy, we contrived to prevent her from oversetting by steering directly before the wind; though not without some difficulty, as, from the little way she made through the water, the waves frequently washed clear over the decks. Besides taking care to keep the vessel steady, we used every precaution to secure our boat from being washed overboard, the loss of which would in our present circumstances be a dreadful misfortune. The cabin, being raised above the level of the main deck, was tolerably clear of water and afforded us some little shelter from the severity of the weather, whither we retired, leaving only one man upon deck to govern the helm, who was fastened by a rope to prevent his being carried away by the waves which at times made a free passage over us.

The gale still continued without remission, the snow falling so thick at the same time as to prevent our seeing to the masthead. We knew from the distance we had run that we could not be far from land. The captain imagined from our course during the night, and since the ship filled in the morning, that we must be near the island of St. John's, which lies between the Magdalen islands and the gulf of Canceau. This gave us hopes of saving our lives in case we could run ashore on some sandy part of it, till they were dashed by the further information we had from the captain that the north-east side of the island was nothing but a continued reef of rocks from one end to the other, and that there was but one harbour where ships could put in, which he recollected was on the opposite side of the island. In a few hours after, we observed the waves grew shorter and break higher, which is always found to be the case on approaching the shore; and likewise a number of gulls and ducks flying about, a further sign we could not be far distant from it.

We now concluded that we were about to run upon the rocks which, the captain informed us, skirted the northeast side of the island, and on approaching the land [we] laboured under greater dread and apprehension than amidst all the dangers we had before experienced, the idea of being cast upon those tremendous rocks being more terrifying than that of being buried, as our companions were, in the bosom of the ocean. The ship had still considerable way through the water, though full, and with no other sail set but a close-reefed fore-top-sail, which was the only one we could display; and the canvas being new, it had hitherto stood the gale. The captain proposed bringing the ship to, to keep her off the land; which I opposed, as well as the mate, urging the probability that we should overset her in the attempt; and that moreover, should we be able to effect it, she must after all drive ashore, as in her present state it was impossible to make any way to windward. Our opinion, however, was rejected, and an attempt was made to brace about the fore yard; but it was found impracticable, the ropes and blocks being covered with ice.

We were therefore obliged to let it remain as before; and the water having suddenly changed its colour, we expected the ship to strike every instant. Small as our expectations were of saving our lives, I thought it incumbent on me to take every precaution to save the dispatches I was charged with, and therefore ordered my servant to open my trunks, and collect all the letters they contained, which I put into a handkerchief and fastened about my waist. He at the same time offered me the money he found in them, to the amount of one hundred and eighty guineas, which I desired him to dispose of as he thought proper, thinking it in the present emergency rather an incumbrance than a matter worthy of preservation. My servant, however, thought otherwise and took care to secure the cash, which was afterwards of more service to us than at that time I could possibly have imagined.

The weather continued thick as usual till about one o'clock when suddenly clearing up, we discovered the land at about three leagues distance. This sight gave us no small satisfaction, taking it at first to be the island of St. John's, which being inhabited by several French and English families, we might have expected some assistance from them; but on a nearer view [we] found, from the plans we had on board, that it had not the least appearance of that island, there being no such mountains and precipices laid down, as we discovered. On drawing nigher, we observed the sea break high, and have a very dismal appearance about three miles from the land (*Margaree Island*).[6] As it was necessary for us to pass through those breakers ere we could gain the shore, we expected that our fate would be determined there; but contrary to our expectations, there was a considerable depth of water, so that we went over the reef without touching, though not without shipping many heavy seas, which, had not the vessel's timbers been strong and the loading light, must infallibly have dashed her to pieces.

The land now began to have a dreadful appearance, seeming at the distance we were off to be high and rocky; but on approaching within a mile of it, we had the pleasure of decrying a fine sandy beach and a bold shore. The sea ran high, but not to such a degree as on the reef we had already passed. As we advanced, the water continued to have a depth beyond our most sanguine wishes, so as to allow us to come within fifty or sixty yards of the beach before we struck. Now was the time for every man's apprehensions to be on the rack, as we might expect on touching the shore that the ship would go to pieces. At length she grounded with a violent concussion. (*The* St. Lawrence *grounded near the mouth of Margaree River. A sandy beach, about a mile in length, here skirts the shore on either side of the channel.*)[7]

On the first stroke the main-mast went out of the step, and on the second the fore-mast; but neither of them fell over the side, the deal boards in the hold being stowed so close together that the masts had no room to play below; at the same time the rudder was unshipped with such violence as to be near killing one of the sailors. As soon as the ship had grounded, the sea began to beat over her in every part, each wave lifting her four or five feet nearer the shore. In a short space of time the stern was beat-in by the sea; and then, having no shelter in the cabin, we were obliged to go upon deck and hang by the shrouds, lest we should be washed overboard. In this uncomfortable situation we remained till the vessel was beat so high by the waves that we could venture to walk upon deck. We now perceived that the ship's keel was broken, which we imagined would occasion her to go to pieces: this however did not happen for the present; which I can only attribute to the boards in the hold being so interwoven with each other, and frozen together by the ice, as to give a degree of solidity to the vessel.

Our first care now was to get out the boat; which was not to be accomplished without difficulty on account of the quantity of ice that was in and about it, and our reduction in number of effective hands by the intoxication of several of the crew, who had thought that the most effectual method of getting rid of the apprehensions they laboured under. Our vessel had, from the violence of the waves dashing against her, broached-to, with her broadside to the wind, so that she afforded some shelter for the boat to the leeward. Having with much labour cleared the boat of ice and prepared her for launching, I ordered some liquor to be distributed to those who were yet sober, and then asked if any were willing to embark with me in the boat and make the attempt to gain the shore. The sea running so high that it appeared scarcely possible for the boat to live in it for a minute, very few were willing to make an experiment so full of risk; so that all who offered themselves were the mate and two sailors, together with my servant and a boy who was a passenger on board.

What gave us the greatest embarrassment in this undertaking was the surf which broke over us every moment, and the intenseness of the cold, which froze every drop of water immediately so as to cover our cloaths with a sheet of ice. At length we got the boat into the water, and having thrown into it an axe and a saw, I leaped in followed by my servant and the mate. The boy followed us, but not springing far enough, fell into the water: he did not however sink immediately; and we contrived to drag him into the boat, but not without difficulty; our fingers being so benumbed with the cold that we had scarcely the power of using them: and this accident was in the issue, by the chill it gave him, of fatal consequence to the unfortunate youth. The two sailors who had agreed to go with us next leaped into the boat; and all the rest seemed ready, notwithstanding their former hesitation, to follow the example, when I found it necessary to shove her off from the ship's side; for, being very small, she certainly would have sunk had so many persons crowded in together. The ship was lying about forty yards from the shore; but before we got half-way to it, we were overtaken by a wave that almost filled the boat, and the next drove us on the dry sand.

TO FIND OURSELVES ONCE MORE safe upon the land gave us no small satisfaction, though in so destitute a state; the joy at having escaped those dangers which so long had been the chief objects of our dread, made us for a few moments forget that we were snatched from them merely to be exposed to others more inevitable; that we had escaped one species of death, probably to undergo another more lingering and painful. What most affected us was the distress of our companions whom we had left on board, whose lamentations and cries for help we could hear very distinctly. But it was impossible for us, however anxious, to afford them any assistance. Our boat being beaten high upon the sand could now be of no use either to us or to them, while the sea was running to such a degree that it was not in the power of a human being to relieve them.

The night was now approaching, and we had not long remained in this situation ere we found ourselves getting stiff with cold; and the gale continuing as severe as ever, we were obliged to wade with extreme difficulty up to our waists in snow, to the shelter of a thick wood about two hundred and fifty yards from the beach. This afforded some relief from the piercing north-west wind; yet a fire was still wanting to warm our frozen limbs, and we had not wherewithal to kindle one.

We had indeed taken the precaution to put a tinder-box in the boat, but the water had rendered it totally useless. Freezing as we stood, there was nothing to be done but to keep the blood in motion by exercise. I therefore recommended it to the men to move about, being better acquainted with the nature of cold climates and that of frost than any of my companions. My advice was strictly adhered to for about half an hour, when the young passenger whom I have already mentioned, being overcome with the severity of the weather, threw himself down in order to sleep; for extreme cold always occasions a sleepy sensation that is not easily to be resisted. I used my utmost endeavour both by persuasion and force to rouse him and make him stand on his legs, but all to no purpose; so I was obliged to let him pursue his inclination.

After walking about for half an hour longer, during which time I felt such a strong desire to sleep that I should have lain down myself, had I not been aware of the fatal consequences attending it, I went to the place where the boy lay, and putting my hand on his face and finding it quite cold, I observed to the mate, who was close by, that I believed he was dead. To which the youth answered immediately that he was not yet dead, but would be so very shortly; and requested I would write, if I survived, to his father at New York, and inform him of the circumstances of his son's misfortune. In about ten minutes we found

THE DEPARTURE

Ensign Prenties and five companions depart Margaree Harbour to search for help, leaving behind the other survivors

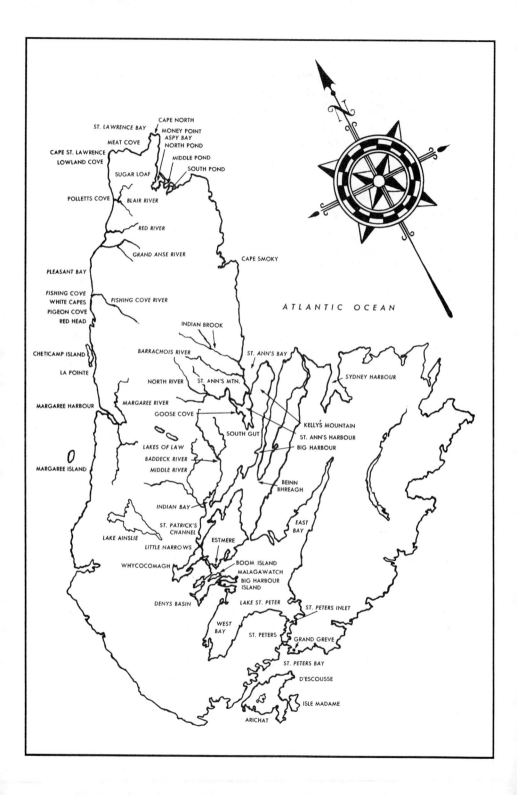

that he had expired, and, as I imagined, without any pain whatever, at least without any acute sensation of it. These trivial matters would be unworthy of notice, but as they serve to show the effect of intense cold on the human body, and to prove that freezing to death is not always attended with so much pain as is commonly supposed.

The death of the boy could not deter the rest of my fellow-sufferers from giving way to this drowsy sensation; and three of them lay down in spite of my repeated exhortations to the contrary. Finding it impossible to keep them on their legs, I broke a branch, and desiring the mate to do the same, our employment during the remainder of the night was to prevent them from sleeping by beating them continually with the branches. This was an exercise useful to ourselves, at the same time that it preserved the lives of our companions. The day-light, which we looked for with such anxious expectation, at length appeared, when I desired the men to pull down their stockings and let me examine their legs, as they observed that they had no feeling in them. As soon as I cast my eyes on them, I perceived very clearly that they were frozen at least half way up; and [I] desired they would immediately rub them with snow, which they did for a considerable time but to little purpose; for it was impossible to restore them to their feeling.

I then went with the mate down to the beach to see if we could discover any traces of the ship and our companions whom we had left on board, and to our great surprise and satisfaction found she had not yet gone to pieces, though the wind continued with unabated severity. My first study now was how to get them ashore, our own safety as well as theirs depending on it. I was almost stiff with cold, but found feeling in every part and was therefore certain I could not be frozen. What seemed greatly to facilitate the undertaking was that the vessel had by this time beat much nigher the shore, so that the distance was but very small at low water.

It was high flood when we arrived on the beach; we were therefore obliged to wait till the tide was out, when we advised the people on board to fasten a rope to the jib-boom, by which they might swing themselves one by one towards the shore. They accordingly adopted this expedient, and by watching the motion of the sea and seizing the opportunity of swinging themselves as the waves retired, they all got safe on the land except a carpenter, who was a passenger in the vessel. He did not think proper to venture in this manner, or was unable, having the night before made rather too free with the bottle. We were happy however to get so many of them on shore, every one of whom, a few hours before, we concluded must have perished.

The captain had fortunately, before he left the ship, put some materials for striking a light in his pocket. We therefore went to work in cutting wood and gathering the branches that lay scattered upon the ground, of which we made a fire with all possible expedition, and were happy for some time in hovering about it and warming our benumbed limbs. Considering the extreme cold we had endured for such a length of time, no luxury could be equal to that of the fire; but this gratification was, like many others, to several of my companions followed by the most excruciating pain as soon as their frozen parts began to thaw. Several of those who had remained all night in the vessel, as well as those who came ashore with me in the boat, had been frozen in different parts of their members. The distress that was now painted in the faces of these unfortunate men, from the tortures they underwent, was beyond expression: this I knew would be the case before I heard them complain; but as there was no remedy, [I] did not think it necessary to give them any intimation of it.

When we came to examine into our numbers, I observed that a Capt. Green, a passenger, was missing; and was informed that he had fallen asleep on board the vessel and had been frozen to death. We were rather uneasy about the man who still remained on board, yet had some hopes of saving his life in case the ship did not go to pieces at the return of low water: but it being too difficult to undertake in the night, we were under the necessity of waiting till the following day. This night we passed a little better than the last; yet, notwithstanding we had a good fire, we found extreme inconveniency from the total want of covering, as well as from hunger, a new misery that we had hitherto been unacquainted with. Besides which, the greatest part of our number were in the most wretched state imaginable from the sores occasioned by the frost.

The next morning, as many of us as were able went to the beach to contrive some means to extricate the carpenter, whose voice we heard on board the vessel. The sea still running with the same violence as before, we could not put out the boat to his assistance, and were therefore obliged to wait the return of low water, when we persuaded him to come on shore in the same manner as the others had done; but this he accomplished with much difficulty, being very weak, and frozen in different parts of his limbs. We still remained without any kind of provisions, and began to be reduced in strength for want of nourishment.

The 7th and 8th the gale continued as boisterous as ever; and in the night between the 8th and 9th of December the ship went to pieces from the stern to the main-mast, from the extreme violence with which the sea broke against her. By this part of her going to pieces, we obtained some provisions which washed on shore, viz. some pieces of salt beef, likewise some fresh meat that hung over the stern, and a quantity of onions that the captain had on board for sale. This relief was very seasonable, it being now the fourth day since we had eaten any kind of provision whatever. Having no utensils, we dressed our meat in the best manner we could, and made what we thought a most delicious repast.

The sense of hunger being assuaged, we set to work in collecting all the provision we could find scattered upon the beach, being apprehensive that we should not soon get a supply from any other quarter. This done, our next care was to get ourselves under cover, and form some kind of shelter from the piercing blast. This task was not an easy one, so many of our company being unable to move, and of the remainder none but the mate and myself capable of any active exertion, being all more or less bitten by the frost; and our number reduced to seventeen by the loss of two persons, as already mentioned. A quantity of deals had floated on shore from the wreck: of these we carried about two hundred and fifty into the wood, and by ten at night completed a kind of house about twenty feet long and ten wide; which was constructed in the following manner. We cut two poles of the above-mentioned length, and, having no nails, tied them at a proper height on the outside of two trees, at the distance of twenty feet from each other: the interval between the poles, which was equal to the breadth of the trees, served for the smoke of our fire to go through; the fire itself being laid in an oblong position, extending itself nearly the whole length of the house. Against these cross poles we placed boards with a slope of about sixty degrees towards the ground, which constituted the two principal sides. The two other sides were composed of boards placed perpendicular, the trunks of the trees being taken in, and forming part of each side: on one of these sides, that looked towards the south-east, we left a vacancy for the entrance.

This business being over, we examined the quantity of provisions we had collected and had the satisfaction to find that we had in store between two and three hundred pounds of salt beef, and a considerable stock of onions. As to bread, we had none; for, when the vessel went to pieces, the casks were stove and the bread lost. Economy and good management were now highly necessary to make our little stock last [as] long as possible, it being quite uncertain when we could get any relief; and in consequence it was determined that each man, whether sick or well, should be confined to a quarter of a pound of beef and four onions per day, as long as the latter should last. This wretched allowance, but just enough to keep a man from starving, was the utmost we thought it prudent to afford ourselves, lest we should be in an uninhabited country; for as yet we were rather uncertain on what coast we were cast away; though afterwards, on comparing circumstances, we concluded it must be on the island of Cape Breton.

ON THE 11th OF DECEMBER, being the sixth day after we landed, the gale abated and gave us an opportunity to launch our boat and get on board what remained of the vessel. Three of us accordingly embarked, having with much labour launched the boat and cleared her of the sand and ice. As soon as we got on board the wreck, we went to work at opening the hatches, and having but one axe, and the cables being frozen over them in a solid lump of ice, it took the whole day to accomplish it. The next day, the weather being still moderate, we went again on board, and having cleared away the remainder of the cable, we cut up part of the deck in order to make room to get out two casks of onions, with a small barrel of beef containing about one hundred and twenty pounds, and three barrels of apples, shipped by a Jewish merchant of Quebec. We likewise found a quarter-cask of potatoes, a bottle of oil, which proved very serviceable to the men's sores, another axe, a large iron pot, two camp kettles, and about twelve pounds of tallow candles. With much difficulty we got this great supply on shore.

On the 13th we made it our business to get our provisions stowed away in a corner of the hut, when, on opening the apple casks, we found their contents, to our great surprise, converted into bottles of Canadian balsam, a more valuable commodity to be sure than apples, but what we could gladly have exchanged in our present situation for something more friendly to the stomach than to the constitution. This disappointment, as may be supposed, extorted a few hearty good wishes towards the Jew; yet we found afterwards some use for his Canadian balsam, though somewhat different from what he intended it should be applied to.

The considerable supply we got from on board the wreck enabled us the next day to add four onions to our daily allowance. We went on board once more on the 14th, and cut as much of the sails as possible from the bowsprit, with part of which we covered our hut and made it tolerably warm and comfortable, notwithstanding the severity of the weather.

By this time the sores of the men who had been frostbitten began to mortify, and caused their toes, fingers, and other parts of the limbs affected, to rot off, their anguish being at the same time almost intolerable. The carpenter, who came on shore after the others, had lost the greatest part of his feet, and on the 14th at night became delirious, in which unhappy state he continued till death released him the following day from his miserable existence. We covered him with snow and branches of trees, having neither spade nor pickaxe to dig a grave for him; nor would it have been possible if we had been provided with them, the ground being in this climate so hard frozen during the winter as to be almost impenetrable. Three days after, our second mate died in the same manner, having been delirous for some hours before he expired.

We felt but very little concern at the death of our companions, either on their account or our own: for in the first place, we considered it rather a happiness than a misfortune to be deprived of life in our present wretched situation, and in the second, because there became the fewer mouths to consume our little stock of provisions: indeed, had not some paid the debt of nature, we should in the end have been reduced to the shocking necessity of killing and devouring one another. Though not yet reduced to this necessity, our condition ws so miserable that it seemed scarcely possible for any new distress to make a sensible addition to it. Besides the prospect of perishing through want in that desolate place, and the pain arising from a perpetual sense of hunger and cold, the agony that the greatest part were in from the sores occasioned by the frost was beyond expression, while their groans were almost equally distressing to the remainder—but what affected me more than all our other miseries, was the quantity of vermin, proceeding from the men's sores, and continually increasing, which infested us in every part and rendered us disgusting even to ourselves. Several, however, who had been but slightly frozen, recovered in a short time with the loss of a few toes and fingers; no one having entirely escaped the frost but myself. On the 20th another sailor died, after having been like the others some time in a delirium, and was buried, or rather covered, in the same manner. Our number was now reduced to fourteen persons; yet we did not think it prudent to increase the allowance of provisions, but still kept it at the rate originally fixed on, of a quarter of a pound of beef *per diem.*

THE MATE AND I HAD FREQUENTLY gone out together since we were shipwrecked, to try if we could discover any traces of inhabitants, but hitherto without success. About a fortnight after we had fixed ourselves in the hut, we took the opportunity of a fine day to walk ten or twelve miles up a river (*Margaree River*),[8] upon the ice, where we observed many tracks of moose-deer and other animals, some of which we might have killed, had we been provided with arms and ammunition. In our progress up the river we discovered several trees cut on one side, as we imagined, by an axe, which gave us reason to think there might be Indians near at hand. On going up to the place we could plainly perceive that there had been some there lately, by their wigwam, which still remained with some fresh bark about it. We likewise found the skin of a moose-deer hanging across a pole.

We travelled a good way further, in hopes of making some more discoveries of this nature; but to no purpose. It gave us nevertheless some satisfaction to find that we were in a place where inhabitants had been lately, as it was probable they might again return there. In case this should happen, I cut a long pole and stuck it in the ice upon the river; then with my knife, which I always took care to preserve, as it was the only one amongst us, cut a piece of bark from a birch tree, and forming it into the shape of a hand with the forefinger extended and pointing towards our hut, fixed it on the top of the pole, and took away the moose-skin, in order that they might perceive that some persons had been on the spot since they left it, and the route they had taken on their return.

We then pursued the way to our habitation and communicated this agreeable information to our companions, who were not yet able to move about; trifling as the hopes were which we could in reason derive from this discovery, yet it gave them considerable satisfaction. Twenty days being elapsed since our shipwreck, and our provisions being very much reduced, I began to entertain a suspicion that there was some foul play during my absence at different times from the hut in search of inhabitants. I was therefore determined to find out the truth, if possible, by keeping a constant watch at night; by which means I at length discovered that the depredators were no other than the captain and two sailors, who had consumed no less than seventy pounds, besides a quantity of onions, in so short a space of time. To prevent such unfair practices for the future, the mate and I never went out together, one of us constantly remaining in the hut.

We continued in a state of suspense from our last discovery for some days, when giving up at length all hopes of seeing any Indians or inhabitants in this place, having provisions only for six weeks longer, and a few of our men together with the captain being recovered, I proposed leaving our habitation with as many as could work in the boat, in search of inhabitants. This proposal was unanimously assented to; but when we came to think how it was to be put in execution, a new difficulty started itself, namely, that of repairing the boat, which had been beat in such a manner by the sea upon the beach that every seam was open.

We first attempted to stop them with dry oakum, but soon found that it would not answer the intended purpose, and having saved no pitch from on board the wreck, we began to despair of the possibility of repairing them. I at length thought of making a kind of succedaneum for pitch of the Canadian balsam, which, as I before mentioned, had been shipped for apples and had been by us brought on shore under that deception. We accordingly went to work in making the experiment, and boiled a quantity of the balsam in the iron kettle we had saved, and frequently taking it off the fire to cool, we soon brought it to a proper consistence. A sufficient quantity of it being prepared, we turned up the boat, and having cleaned her bottom, gave her a coat of the balsam, which effectually stopped up all crevices for the present. This done, we got a small sail rigged to a mast, which shipped and unshipped occasionally; and then pitched upon the persons who were to go with me in the boat.

By the 1st of January, with much difficulty and fatigue, we got our boat in tolerable condition so that she could swim without making much water; likewise our mast and sail rigged, in case we should happen to get a fair wind, which we could not often expect on this coast at the present season of the year; for, during the winter months, it blows almost constantly from west to north-west, which is immediately on the land. We could not expect therefore to have much occasion for our sail, nevertheless it might sometimes be serviceable, and afford some relief to the rowers. We had agreed to take six in the boat, viz. the captain and mate, two sailors, myself and servant: of the others none were so far recovered as to be judged equal to the fatigues we might expect in this expedition.

Our shoes being all nearly worn out, my employment during the whole of the next day was to make a kind of *mowkisins*, or Indian shoes, of canvas. My needle was nothing more than the handle of a pewter spoon, which I had fashioned as well as I could for the purpose, and the same canvas supplied me with thread. As soon as I had made twelve pair, which was two for each man in our party, we divided the provisions that remained into fourteen equal parts, which amounted only to a quarter of a pound of beef per day for six weeks; those who were to stay behind sharing as much as we who were to go in the boat, notwithstanding the great fatigue which we had every reason to expect.

EVERY NECESSARY PRELIMINARY being adjusted, we proposed setting off the next day; but the wind blowing fresh at north-west [we] were obliged to remain where we were till the 4th. By this time the ice, floating in prodigious quantities on the coast, and in some places collecting and blocking up the bays, rendered our undertaking extremely hazardous; yet we thought it more advisable to face any danger and to encounter any hardship than to remain in our present situation with a certainty of starving.

In the afternoon of the 4th, the wind moderating, we got our provisions and whatever little matters might be of service to us into the boat; and, having taken leave of our companions, set off on our expedition. Having got about eight miles from the place of our shipwreck, the wind began to increase and blow very hard from the south-east, which was immediately off the shore. The boat as well as the oars being none of the best, we were on the point of being blown out to sea, but by the dint of rowing made shift to get into a deep bay about a mile ahead, where we thought we might pass the night with safety. (*This is the bay formed by La Pointe, the southern tip of Chéticamp Island, and the curving beach that joins the island to the mainland. La Pointe is eleven miles distant from the mouth of Margaree River.*)[9]

Having got everything on shore, we hauled our boat up as high as our strength would permit so as to prevent the sea from doing her any damage. This done, we set to work in lighting our fires and cutting our wood for the night: we likewise cut some pine-branches, the smaller of which served us to lie on, and the larger, in the form of a wigwam, to shelter us from the inclemency of the weather.

The place we had landed on was a fine sandy beach, with little or no snow on it. Having observed some small pieces of wood cast on shore by the tide, that had formerly been cut with an axe, a number of long poles scattered along the edge of the bank, which had likewise been cut in the same manner, I thought it likely there might be some inhabitants near at hand; and proposed, as soon as we had taken a little refreshment, to go along the beach to a high point of land at about two miles' distance, which was

clear of wood and appeared to be cultivated; thinking
from thence we might make some useful discoveries.

I accordingly set out soon after with two of the men;
and before we had proceeded a mile, saw the remains of a
shallop or Newfoundland fishing-boat, almost covered
with sand, which seemed to have been set on fire. This
gave us hopes of discovering something else to our satisfaction, and we proceeded as fast as we could to the point
of land. Having gained the top of it, we descried to our in-
expressible joy a few houses about half a mile distant, towards which we directed our course, having no doubt but
that we should now meet with some relief; but on coming
up to them, found they were only the remains of some old
store-houses, which had been built there for the curing of
cod-fish, and to all appearance had been abandoned some
years before.

This was a mortifying disappointment to us. We determined however to make the most of our discovery; and observing a number of old casks lying about in different
parts, we searched them as well as the houses very minute-
ly, in hopes of finding some provisions; but to no purpose.
As we walked along the point, we gathered about a quart
of cranberries, some of which we ate, preserving the remainder for our companions. Having reconnoitred every
part of this point, without any further success, we returned to our boat, and communicating the discoveries we
made to our companions, gave them their share of the ber-
ries we had gathered. Even these discoveries gave us much
satisfaction, as they tended to confirm our hopes of finding some inhabitants in the course of our voyage along the
coast.

In the meantime, the wind came round to the north-
west, and blew with such violence as to prevent us from
proceeding on our voyage. It continued so for two days,

when, happening to get up in the middle of the night, I was astonished on observing, while the wind continued blowing as hard as ever, that the sea was entirely without agitation. I immediately awoke the mate to inform him of this extraordinary phaenomenon; and going down to the beach together to know the cause, we found the sea all covered with ice, nothing but a large sheet of it being to be seen for leagues around. This was an alarming circumstance, as it seemed to preclude all possibility of proceeding any farther, and might give us cause even to regret having left our habitations: for, though we were so near, it was impossible to return by land, besides other impediments, on account of the depth of snow, which was impassable unless with snow-shoes.

The wind continued to blow from the same quarter for two days longer; at length, on the 9th, it became perfectly calm. Next morning the wind came round to the southeast, which was directly off the land, and in a short time blew extremely hard, so that by four o'clock in the afternoon there was not a piece of ice to be seen along the coast, the whole of it being blown out to sea. This was a very pleasing sight to us, as it gave us a prospect of being extricated from our present dreary situation. However, the violence of the wind prevented us from moving till the 11th of January, when the weather being moderate, and a fine light breeze blowing along the coast, we launched our boat with much difficulty, being greatly reduced in strength for want of a due degree of nourishment. Having got round the clear point of the land, we hoisted our sail and put before the wind.

The weather being very moderate, and little or no sea running, we made tolerable way, and had not proceeded far before we described an extremely high point (*Cap Rouge, Red Cape*), about seven leagues ahead, with a continued precipice along the coast, so that it was impossible for us to land on any part of it before we came to that head-land. This made it very dangerous to attempt the passage; for if the wind should happen to come round to the north-west, we must infallibly have perished amongst the rocks.

But danger was no longer an object to be considered by us; so we got out two oars, not being able to use any more, as the boat had been so much damaged that two men were constantly employed in keeping her clear of water, and with the assistance of a fair wind made the point about eleven o'clock at night; but finding no place that we could possibly land on, we were obliged to keep along the coast till two in the morning, when the wind increasing, and a stony beach appearing, on which we should not have thought it expedient to land had the wind been moderate, we were obliged to put ashore, and immediately got our provisions out of the boat. The beach was of some height from the surface of the water, the sea having beat the gravel up into a kind of bank; which rendered it impossible for us to haul our boat up. We were therefore obliged to leave her to the mercy of the sea.

The place where we landed was a beach of about four hundred yards in length, bounded at the distance of about fifty yards from the water's edge by a precipice of at least one hundred feet in height, which inclosed it on all sides. (*Now called Pigeon Cove, it is fourteen and a half miles straight distance from La Pointe. Allowing for coastal contours, Prenties' estimated distance of seventeen and a half miles is about right.*)[10] If the wind should come round to the north-west, we knew that we should be entirely deprived of shelter, yet, as it blew too fresh for us to attempt putting to sea again, we were obliged to remain there, notwithstanding these inconveniences.

On the 13th the wind came round to the north-west, and blowing very hard, the sea beat with such violence against the shore as to drive our boat twenty yards higher than she was, and to beat several holes in her bottom. Now was the time for us to feel all the miseries of our present situation; for being surrounded by precipices which prevented us from sheltering ourselves in the woods, and having so little covering, and no firing but what we collected from some pieces of timber which floated accidentally upon the shore, we could but just keep ourselves from absolute freezing. The same weather continued for eight days with a prodigious fall of snow, a circumstance that added to our other inconveniences.

At length, on the 21st, the weather became more moderate, and the snow ceased; having in the course of this last week fallen to the depth of three feet perpendicular. This gave us an opportunity of cooking our provisions, which we had done but once since our landing. Even this was a great loss to us, as the water that the meat was boiled in afforded us almost as much nourishment as the meat itself.

Next day we contrived with much labour to turn our boat half-way over, in order to examine the damage she had received, which we found considerable; the coat of balsam being entirely rubbed off, and several holes made in her bottom. We expected the ice would go to sea as it had done once before, whenever the wind should come round to the southward; and therefore thought, if we could but get our boat repaired, that we might still have some chance of meeting with inhabitants. But the great difficulty was how to repair it; for we had no pitch or balsam left, and but little dry oakum, which was of no service to us without the former. After trying various methods, we at last gave it up as a thing entirely impracticable, and began to turn our thoughts towards some other means of getting out of this bleak and barren place, to search for relief in an inhabited country.

THOUGH IT WAS IMPOSSIBLE for us to climb the precipice by which we were encompassed, yet, if we were determined to abandon our boat, we imagined that we might easily get in to the woods by walking along shore upon the ice, which still covered the sea and had strength sufficient to bear any weight. In fact the mate and I proposed walking a few miles on it, in order to make the experiment. We accordingly set out, and had not proceeded far before we came to the entrance of a river (*Fishing Cove River*)[11] and a fine sandy beach, where, had our good fortune directed us to land, we might have lived more comfortably and have preserved our boat.

But what was to be done now that we could get into the woods? We could not think of walking across them in search of a cultivated country: besides that we should be entirely ignorant how to direct our course, the depth of snow, which had by this time increased to six feet in the woods, rendered it impossible for us to travel without snow-shoes. After consulting together, we at last came to a resolution of taking the next day what provisions we had upon our backs, and coasting along the ice, till we could discover some inhabitants, expecting, from its present appearance of strength, that it would remain for some time longer: and the wind having drifted the greatest part of the snow off it, we computed that we should be able to walk about ten miles a day, even in our present weak and reduced condition.

This being fully resolved, we were to set out the morning of the 24th; but on the night preceding it, the wind came round to the south-east and blew hard, attended with snow and rain; so that in the morning, as I already apprehended would be the case, the whole sheet of ice which the night before looked so firm was demolished or driven out to sea. Thus were all our schemes frustrated— neither ice to walk on, nor boat to carry us through the water; not even a possibility of moving from this place where we were embayed and surrounded by insurmountable precipices. Thus circumstanced, we were again obliged to turn our thought towards some scheme for repairing our boat: upon that our only hope depended.

We had plenty of oakum to stop up the holes and seams, but nothing to substitute in the room of pitch, to prevent the water from penetrating. I at length thought of a plan which I imagined might have the wished-for effect, namely, that of throwing water over the oakum and letting it freeze into a cake of ice. As soon as day appeared, I resolved to put this scheme to the test, and having cleared the boat of snow and gravel, immediately went to work. The men in general made light of my undertaking and assisted with much reluctance, thinking that they were throwing away their labour. However, I soon convinced them to the contrary; for by four o'clock in the afternoon, by continually throwing water over the oakum, we froze up every seam and hole in such a manner that not a drop of water could enter as long as the weather continued freezing, as at present.

On the 27th of January, the weather being moderate, and a light breeze directly off the shore, we got our boat very carefully launched, and set off early in the morning from this ill-omened bay. We had the pleasure to observe that the boat made little or no water, so that we were enabled to keep our four oars continually at work. As we advanced along the coast, we found it still bordered by nothing but barren precipices, with every four or five miles perhaps a small sandy beach.

The weather continued very moderate all the day of the 27th, so that by six o'clock in the evening we computed that we had rowed about twelve miles from where we departed in the morning. This indeed would be but an indifferent days' work for people in health and vigour, but a great deal for those in our circumstances; not only being extremely weakened and reduced, but the boat itself being very heavy and unwieldy from the quantity of ice in it. We put ashore about six o'clock upon a small sandy beach (*probably the beach on Pleasant Bay through which the Grand Anse River enters the ocean, although the distance from Pigeon Cove is not more than six and a half miles*),[12] and by placing oars under our boat, dragged her carefully some yards from the water; so that she lay very safe while the wind continued as it then was. We next cut some branches, and having made a fire, sheltered ourselves as well as possible in the wood. Our tinder being nearly consumed, I was obliged to furnish a fresh supply by cutting away the back part of my shirt, which I had worn ever since we left the ship.

A shower of rain the next day unfortunately melted all the ice off our boat: we were therefore prevented from going any farther till a return of the frost, and had the mortification to lose the benefit of a fine day, in the course of which we might have proceeded with a good boat several leagues more on our journey. What made the matter worse was that our provisions were now reduced to two pounds and a half of beef for each man.

On the morning of the 29th, the mate having wandered a little distance from our fire, returned in haste to inform me that he had discovered a partridge perched on the bough of a tree, which he thought I might possibly devise some method of catching. I immediately went to the place where he had seen it, and found it in the same situation as before. Observing that the bird was very tame, and not above fourteen feet from the ground, I cut down a long pole, and taking part of the rope-yarn that fastened my canvas shoes, made a running loop of it and fixed it to the end of the pole; then walking softly under the tree, and lifting the pole gently up, I fixed the loop about the partridge's neck, and giving it a sudden jerk, closed the loop and secured the bird. The mate, as well as myself, as soon as I had caught it, laughed very heartily for the first time that either of us had any inclination to smile since our shipwreck. We then went towards the fire with our prize, and boiled it in some melted snow together with a little salt water, to give the broth a relish: having divided it when dressed into six equal parts, and cast lots for the choice of each, we sat down to what we found a delicious meal; the only one, excepting the quart of cranberries, for which we were indebted to chance or Providence since we had been cast upon the island.

ON THE AFTERNOON OF THE 29th it began to freeze hard, we took the advantage of the frost to stop the boat's leaks as before; and the wind still continuing moderate, we launched her as soon as that business was completed and put to sea. The day being almost spent before we set off, we could not make above seven miles to a sandy beach and thick wood, which seemed to afford a tolerable shelter. (*This may have been at the mouth of Otter Brook.*) In this place we passed the night; and the next day, the weather being still favourable, we launched our boat betimes in the morning, in order to get before night as far as possible on our journey; but we had not proceeded above six miles, before the wind freshening up from the southeast, obliged us to put ashore and haul up our boat. (*Polletts Cove. The distance from the beach on Pleasant Bay is eleven and a half miles, which accords well with Prenties' estimate of thirteen miles for two days' travel.*) [13]

A heavy fall of rain, which continued the whole day rendered our situation extremely uncomfortable and melted again the icy calking of the boat. We were therefore to console ourselves as well as we could, in the certainty of remaining here till a return of the frost, and meanwhile proposed to reconnoitre, as far as our reduced state would allow us, into the country. In this however we were prevented by the quantity of snow which still lay on the ground, and was not yet sufficiently frozen to bear our weight without rackets or snow-shoes. Towards the spring of the year in these cold climates, they may for the most part be dispensed with, when the snow has become more condensed by its own weight, the influence of the sun, and the rains which begin to fall at this season. The frost then returning, after the thaw, forms a kind of incrustation on the surface that will bear a man's weight without sinking. Had this season been arrived, we should have abandoned our crazy boat, and, taking the little provision we still possessed, have made an attempt to discover inhabitants by a march into the heart of the country; perhaps it was fortunate we could not attempt it, as in all probability we should have perished in the woods.

Not having it in our power to wander towards any other part, we walked along the shore as far as we were able, and saw nothing that could attract our notice but some stumps of trees, from which the trunks might have been cut some years before: from this curcumstance we could collect no very sanguine hope of being near an inhabited country. Soon after, the wind coming round to the northwest and bringing the frost along with it, we were once more enabled to repair our boat and to prepare for launching it, as soon as the wind should abate its violence. This happening in some degree on the 1st of February, we immediately embarked and pursued our coasting voyage; but the severity of the cold having formed a quantity of ice, it was with extreme labour that we contrived to get five miles before night, one of our party being employed in breaking the ice with a pole, and clearing it from the bows of the boat.

The following day, the wind blowing fresh from the north-west quarter prevented us again from proceeding any farther till the 3rd, when, coming round to the west, which is directly along the shore and the most favourable that could blow for us, we were enabled to embark and pursue our voyage. Our boat, notwithstanding all our diligence in calking, made now so much water that we were obliged to keep one man constantly at work in bailing it out with a camp kettle. The wind, however, was as fair as we could wish, and being neither too slack nor too violent, we for some time went at the rate of four miles an hour, with the assistance of our oars; but soon after, the wind increasing, we laid in our oars, and ran under our sail alone at the rate of about five miles an hour.

After having run about sixteen miles (*at this point, ten miles in straight distance from Polletts Cove, the castaways rounded Cape St. Lawrence and caught a distance view of Cape North*)—we discovered an exceeding high land, about six leagues distant, with several other mountains and large bays between us; and it being yet early in the day, [with] a fine wind and no great sea, we were in hopes if the wind should not increase too much, that we should be able to reach it before night. As we proceeded along the coast, we found it in every part high and rocky, which made us very uneasy lest the wind should rise before we could make the head-land. About two o'clock in the afternoon, when we supposed we were within three leagues of it, we discovered an island about twenty miles from the main; and, on comparing circumstances, we concluded that the island must be that of St. Paul (*fifteen miles distant from Cape North*), and the high land the north point of Cape Breton. The prodigious height of the land led us into an erroneous computation of its distance; for, notwithstanding we had supposed that we were within three leagues of it when we first discovered the island of St. Paul, we found before we reached it that we had run near five leagues. (*Cape North is just short of nine miles distant from Cape St. Lawrence. The indentation of Meat Cove, and the deeper indentation of St. Lawrence Bay, would add miles for a boat creeping along the shore. Prenties' estimate of twelve and a half miles may be conservative.*)

It was almost dark by the time we reached the North Cape; where finding no place to land, we were obliged to double the cape and continue our journey. The wind now began to freshen, and we had a heavy sea from the north-east to encounter as soon as we came opposite to the cape. After having doubled it, our course lay in a very different direction from what it had been in the morning; so that we were obliged to strike our sail, and take to the oars. The wind at the same time blew so hard off the high lands, that it was with the utmost difficulty we could keep along the coast; had we not been assisted by a heavy swell that came from the north-east, we must certainly have been blown out to sea.

Finding no place to land during the night, we continued rowing as close as we could to the rocks till about five in the morning; when hearing the sea run on the shore very long and heavy, we imagined that we must be off a sandy beach. We accordingly rowed towards the land, and at the distance of fifty yards, for it was yet dark, were able to discern a beach at least four miles in length. It was not however a convenient place for us to put in, on account of the surf and a long and heavy sea that rolled on it; yet being so much fatigued with rowing that we were incapable of proceeding any farther, we were obliged to attempt a landing. This we effected with more ease than we looked for, and suffered no other inconvenience but that of having our boat nearly filled with water on the beach. (*The castaways landed at the end of the long beach in Aspy Bay, near where a monument marks the supposed landing place of John Cabot.*)[14]

Having landed, our first care was to haul up the boat, that she might meet with no further damage from the sea. We then got into the woods, which lay close to the shore; and as I had taken the precaution to put our tinder-box in my bosom before we landed, to preserve it from the water, we contrived to kindle a fire; a refreshment we had much occasion for, having got wet in landing, and being in so weak and reduced a condition that it was with the greatest difficulty we could keep ourselves awake for a few minutes when before the fire; so that we were under the necessity of watching in turn; lest, all being asleep together, the fire should go out and we should be frozen to death. Having now time to consider every circumstance, and finding as soon as daylight appeared, that the land still continued to have an opposite bearing to that on the other side of the point, we had no doubt remaining but that we were upon the North Cape of the island of Breton, which, together with Cape Ray on the island of Newfoundland, marks the entrance of the Gulf of St. Lawrence.

Our provisions were now entirely consumed, and having not the most distant prospect of getting any more, we were ready to abandon ourselves to despair. As we were certain of being on an inhabited island, we might have flattered ourselves with hopes of getting relief by persevering in our dilatory progress, had we wherewithal to provide for our immediate subsistence. Having weighed the necessity of the case, and the misery of perishing by hunger, I was of the opinion, as well as the mate, that it would be most advisable to sacrifice one for the preservation of the rest; and that the most proper method would be by casting lots, [to decide] which should be the unfortunate victim. But this shocking, though prudent, resolution we agreed to put off to the last extremity.

We had not been able to secure our boat so effectually but that the sea had beat her higher up on the beach, and filled her with sand. We were obliged therefore to set two of the men to work in clearing her, and afterwards in stopping the leaks, as already described; while the remainder of our party were detached by different routes along the shore, to see if they could find any kind of provision.

The mate and myself travelled along the sandy beach till we were prevented from going any further by an inlet of water, when we were a good deal surprised to observe the tide ebb and flow every ten minutes. (*This phenomenon can best be observed when the streams flowing into North Pond are in flood.*) We were not however at present in a disposition to pay much regard to this or any other extraordinary appearance of nature; and seeing a great quantity of oyster shells lying upon the shore, we searched them diligently, in hopes of finding some that were full; but without success. This again made us curse our destiny, that we should have been cast away on so barren and miserable a country, and in such an unlucky time of the year, when we were not only deprived of the relief we might have got at any other season, from the natural productions of the earth; but when even the animals, inhabitants of both elements, had retired to their holes and hiding places, to shield themselves from the intense cold which prevails during the winter in this inhospitable climate.

We still continued our search, notwithstanding the ill success we had hitherto experienced, and contrived at length to gather about two quarts of hips, or wild rose buds, by throwing up the snow and searching in different parts of the bank. Having with this sorry food allayed in some degree the keen sense of hunger, and the wind having become somewhat more moderate, we got into our boat and pushed off, the day being already drawing towards a conclusion. Our progress was however soon impeded by the quantity of ice that floated upon the water; which obliged us to put ashore on another part of the same beach. In landing I had the misfortune to let the tinder-box fall from my bosom into the water, by which means we were unable to kindle a fire; and being exceedingly wet, as was generally the case when we landed, we were in this place in a most uncomfortable situation, and suffered much from the cold. We therefore thought it best to get into our boat again as fast as possible, and return to the spot from whence we came, in hopes of finding some fire still remaining.

It was with the greatest difficulty we got back, being the whole way under the necessity of breaking through the ice, which had by this time formed almost into a solid sheet. We were very anxious lest our fire should mean-while have gone out, and thought it a lucky circumstance we had not been able to go any farther from it. On our ar-rival at the place, we had the satisfaction to find it was not totally extinguished: had this been the case, we must have perished in the course of the night. The fire being re-paired, I cut up the remainder of my shirt to make some more tinder; and, as the damage it got had nearly proved so fatal to us, was resolved to be more particular in my care of it for the future. (*Hereafter Prenties does not al-ways give his day-to-day estimate of distance covered. As a result, only the last campsüte, on St. Ann's Bay, can be located, and this with no great accuracy.*)

ON THE 8th OF FEBRUARY, the wind came round to the south-west, which cleared off the ice and enabled us to leave this place by ten o'clock in the morning. As we pro-ceeded along the shore, we found it was not quite so rocky as it had been on the other side of the north cape. We were therefore able to land this night without difficulty within a large rock, by which we were sheltered from the wind and sea. We were here very comfortably situated in every respect, except our want of provisions. The next day, the weather continuing moderate, we had again proceeded about eight miles on our journey, when the wind beginning to blow so hard as to raise a considerable swell, we were obliged to steer to the shore; and in landing had the misfortune to lose two of our oars, which were washed overboard by the surf.

On the following day the wind lulled; and we immediately took the advantage of it to put to sea. We had now but two oars remaining; which being doubled-manned, we contrived to get about six miles before night. This was a very hard day's work, considering our present weak condition; for having been a length of time without tasting any kind of nourishment, we were so much reduced in strength, that when we got on shore, we could scarcely walk for fifty yards together.

The weather being unfavourable on the 11th, we were under the necessity of remaining the whole day in the same resting place; and having leisure to search about the shore, we were fortunate enough to find a few rose buds, which we esteemed at present a great delicacy. Had we not met with this supply, it would have been absolutely requisite to put our above mentioned scheme into execution. We thought ourselves extremely unlucky in not having found, in the course of our wanderings, so much as the body of any dead animal: nor, except the partridge, did we see any live one that we had the smallest chance of capturing. At different times we had hopes of catching some of the otters that we frequently saw on the ice, particularly on the small rivers and inlets: but we never found them at any distance from the holes which they continually kept open, to give themselves a free passage in and out of the water. We likewise discovered at different times some beavers' houses; but could not ensnare any of the animals.

On the 12th the wind became moderate, and we proceeded once more on our journey. The coast seemed to diminish in height as we passed along it, which made us hope we were now approaching the cultivated part of the island. Next day the weather got milder, with a fall of rain: so that it was with difficulty we could get our boat to swim, the ice thawing gradually off the bottom. This obliged us to put ashore long before night; and when we had landed and made a fire, we found no other immediate want but that of provisions, having consumed all the hips or rose buds that we had gathered at out last landing place.

Having reconnoitred very carefully all around, and searched in every part under the snow, we were not able to procure ourselves even that miserable sustenance. Being now driven to the last extremity, we were obliged to sacrifice our prospect of travelling any farther to the immediate preservation of our lives. About a dozen tallow candles remained, which we had hitherto employed in stopping the leaks of our boat, as fast as she sprung one in any particular place. Of these we divided a small part among us; which gave us some relief for the present. The two following days we coasted for a few miles, searching for a place where we could meet with some hips; but our search proved ineffectual. This was the only kind of food we could now expect; and had we discovered any place that abounded with them, it was our intention to draw up the boat there, and remain till they were consumed.

We began now to be fully sensible of our desperate situation, and to expect that our fate would be that of perishing with hunger. Notwithstanding that idea was horrid enough, yet what gave me the most uneasiness was that my friends would probably forever remain uninformed of our wretched catastrophe. It may appear to those who have not been in similar circumstances that this would take up but a small part of one's reflection, in comparison with the dread of such a death; yet, however it might have been with the rest of my companions, it was that idea that chiefly preyed upon my spirits. In order to prevent it as far as possible, I took every occasion of cutting out my name on the bark of the largest trees. The fatigue of cutting it, as well as the preservation of my knife, which I observed before was the only one amongst us, would not allow me to be more particular. But on the walls of the store-houses which we had discovered in the beginning of our progress, I wrote a short account of our disasters in English and French, and requested, if any persons should fall in with it, that they would transmit it to my father at Quebec.

ON THE 17th, WE MADE ANOTHER DIVISION of a part of the tallow candles that yet remained; and on the following day, the wind being favourable, we proceeded about five miles; where finding a fine, flat country,[15] and a sandy beach that extended for a considerable way, and being so much debilitated that we knew it would be impossible for us to go much farther, we put on shore with a determined resolution to perish on this place, unless some unforeseen accident should bring us relief. To attempt drawing up our boat would in our present weak condition be a vain undertaking, so we were obliged to leave her exposed to the mercy of the sea. All that we could preserve was our axe, a saw, and the sail of the boat, which we generally made use of as a covering.

As soon as we landed, we made it our business to clear away the snow from a particular spot in the entrance of the wood, where we intended to remain; and having cut some small branches of pine to lie upon, together with some larger to serve for a shelter, which we stuck into the bank of snow that surrounded us, we made our fire. This done, we all went in search of hips, and had the good fortune to find about a pint of them, which, boiled up with a couple of tallow candles, afforded us a tolerable meal.

The next day we passed without any kind of provision, and being apprehensive that our little remaining strength would soon desert us, we employed ourselves in cutting and piling as much wood as we were able, to supply the fire. Meanwhile the waves had beat our boat so high upon the beach, as to be quite dry as soon as the wind subsided, and to deprive us of the power of putting to sea again, had we been disposed to do it: for our strength was by no means equal to the task of moving her a single foot.

We again employed the whole day of the 19th in search of hips: but it was not attended with any success. Our tallow candles were therefore the only resource we had left, and by this time they became reduced to two. We found ourselves so much weakened the following day, that we could make no further use of our axe, and were under the necessity of creeping about in our turns to gather for our fire the rotten branches of trees, that lay scattered upon the ground. As we had not a proper quantity of fuel, the fire that we kept up was but just sufficient to preserve us from freezing: for, though the season was so far advanced towards the spring, yet, excepting some particular days, the weather was as cold as in the month of December.

Having now no more than two tallow candles remaining, and finding no longer a possibility of gathering any hips, being too weak even to search for them, we thought it likely that we might derive some degree of nourishment from the kelpweed, of which there was a quantity lying upon the shore. We accordingly collected a little of it, and with melted snow boiled it for a few hours in a kettle; but, at the conclusion, found it very little tenderer than at first. We then melted one of our tallow candles in the liquor, and having supped it up and eat a quantity of the weed, our appetite became somewhat satiated: but in about two hours time we were all affected with a very uneasy sensation and were soon after seized with a fit of vomiting, without being able to bring the offending matter entirely off the stomach. This fit of vomiting having continued for about four hours, we found ourselves tolerably easy, but at the same time exceedingly exhausted.

On the 22nd we made use of some more kelpweed and our last tallow candle. It still operated in the same manner, but not to so violent a degree as it had done before. The next day the wind blew very moderate from the north-west, and brought a severe frost along with it. We had now an opportunity to repair our boat; and, if our strength had been sufficient to launch it into the water, we should have changed our resolution, and have quitted the place. We made indeed a faint attempt to launch the boat; but, on finding that we could not move her an inch from where she lay upon the shore, we were obliged to give over the design. Our candles being all consumed, we were under the necessity of boiling the kelpweed without the mixture of tallow, which, however nauseous at any other time, afforded us then, not only some kind of nourishment, but even an exquisite relish.

Having for three days tasted of no other food but the kelpweed, we began to swell to an alarming degree. This we were at a loss whether to attribute to the kelpweed, or to the cold (for we were not able to keep a sufficient fire): however I thought then, and do still believe, that it proceeded from the former; for, notwithstanding we had often before been exposed to the utmost severity of the frost, and sometimes without any shelter whatever, yet we had never found ourselves affected with this extraordinary symptom; but, on the contrary, were as much reduced in bulk as we were in strength: whereas in a few days, the swelling had increased to such a degree all over our bodies, that, notwithstanding the little flesh we had upon our bones, we could sink our fingers two inches deep on the skin; the impression of which remained visible for above an hour after. Hunger nevertheless still obliged us to make use of the kelpweed. I have never since consulted with any naturalist or physician about the extraordinary effects of this weed; yet doubt not but they may be accounted for from natural causes.[16]

We passed a few days more in the same manner; at the expiration of which we were so much swollen, as to be almost deprived of our sight, and so reduced in strength that it was with the utmost difficulty we could keep our fire in by crawling about in turn, and breaking the rotten branches that lay scattered upon the snow. The time was now arrived, when I thought it highly expedient to put the plan before mentioned into execution; but on feeling the pulse of my companions, found that some of them were rather averse to the proposal; the desire of life still prevailing above every other sentiment, notwithstanding the wretched condition they were in, and the impossibility even of preserving it by any other method.

I thought it an extraordinary instance of infatuation that men should prefer the certainty of a lingering and miserable death, to the distant chance of one more immediate and less painful. However, on consulting with the mate what was to be done, I found that though they objected to the proposal of casting lots which should be the victim, yet all concurred in the necessity of someone being sacrificed for the preservation of the rest. The only question was how it should be determined; when, by a reasoning more agreeable to the dictates of self-love than of justice, it was agreed on that, as the captain was now so exceedingly reduced as to be evidently the first who would sink under our present complicated misery; as he had been the person to whom we considered ourselves in some measure indebted for all our misfortunes; and further, as he had, ever since our shipwreck, been the most remiss in his exertions towards the general good, he was undoubtedly the person who should be first sacrificed.

I must confess that I thought at that time there was some colour of truth in this conclusion: yet I was not a little shocked at the captain's intended fate, although I had more reason than anyone else to be incensed against him, not only on account of his neglect of duty and his malpractices at the hut in purloining our provisions, but for another reason likewise. After our shipwreck, I had discovered by some papers which had been washed on shore, that, though the captain's pretended destination was to New York, yet his real one was to the West Indies, if he could possibly effect it. Thus would he have baffled General Haldimand's intentions in sending me with dispatches, that might be of the first consequence to this country; and not only have disappointed, but also have defrauded me of the money which I paid him for my passage.

THE DETERMINATION NOW MADE was kept secret from the captain; and it would have been impossible for us to live many days longer without putting it into execution, had we not happily met with relief from a quarter whence we little expected it. On the 28th of February, as we were lying about our fire, we thought that we heard the sound of human voices in the woods; and soon after discovered two Indians, with guns in their hands, who did not seem yet to have perceived us. This sight gave us fresh strength and spirits; so, getting up, we advanced towards them with the greatest eagerness imaginable.

As soon as we were perceived by the Indians, they started back and seemed fixed for a few moments to the ground with surprise and horror. This indeed is not to be wondered at, when it is considered that, besides the amazement they must naturally have felt on suddenly meeting with white men in this uninhabited part of the island, our appearance itself was enough to alarm the most intrepid: our cloaths being almost entirely burnt off, so that we were bare in several parts of our bodies, our limbs swollen to a prodigious bulk, our eyes from the same cause almost invisible, and our hair in a confused and dishevelled state about our heads and shoulders, particularly of those who wore it long; for we had not been able to comb it since our shipwreck. As we advanced towards the Indians, some of us wept, while other laughed, through joy. Being a little recovered from their surprise, they did not show much inclination to accost us, till I got up to one of them and took him by the hand; when he shook it for some time very heartily; the usual mode of salutation among the Indians.

They began at length to show marks of compassion at our distressed appearance; and I imagine their shyness at first proceeded from the repugnance which it naturally inspired: for, these Indians being converted to Christianity, I will not attribute it to a motive so contrary to that doctrine, as the idea of the trouble they might expect, without any compensation, in relieving us. They then walked with us to our fire and, sitting down by it together, one of them who could speak a little broken French desired we would inform him when we came, and the particulars of the accident that brought us there. I accordingly gave him as concise an account as possible of the disasters and fatigues we had undergone: during the relation, he seemed to be very much affected at our sufferings.

Having finished my narration, I asked the Indian if he could furnish us with any kind of provisions; to which he answered in the affirmative. Observing that we had very little fire, he suddenly started up and took our axe in his hand; when looking at it and laughing heartily, I suppose at the badness of it, he threw it down again, and taking his tomahawk from his side, which is a small hatchet that the Indians always carry about them, he went, and in a short time cut a quantity of wood, which he brought and threw upon our fire. This done, he took up his gun, and, without saying a word, went off with his companion.

This would have been a very alarming circumstance to persons ignorant of the Indian manners; but I was so well acquainted with the humour of these people, who seldom speak when there is not an absolute occasion for it, that I doubted not but they were gone for some provisions, and that we should see them again very shortly. Notwithstanding the length of time we had been without nourishment, I must confess that I felt but little inclination to eat: the fire which the Indian had made was the greatest refreshment to us, as we had been for many days without a good one.

After about three hours had elapsed, during which interval some of our party were not without anxiety lest the Indians should never return, we perceived them coming round a point at a small distance in a bark canoe. (*This point is the end of the long beach that separates St. Ann's Harbour from St. Ann's Bay. It was on this beach that the Indians found and rescued St. Luc de La Corne in 1761.*)[17]

Being arrived and landed upon the beach, they took out of their canoe some smoaked venison and a bladder of seal oil, which they brought up to our fire-place: having put some of the meat into our kettle, they boiled it in melted snow, and then gave each of us a very small quantity of it together with some oil. I knew very well their reason for being so sparing of their meat; for eating a quantity of gross food in our present state might be attended with the most fatal consequences. It gave me no small pleasure to find that the Indians were so careful of us.

This light repast being ended, the Indians desired three of us to embark in their canoe, that being all she could carry at a time, and proceed from this place to their hut, which lay five miles farther by water and about a mile from the shore in the middle of the woods. (*The Indian encampment was situated inland from the end of Goose Cove, an indentation of St. Ann's Harbour.*)[18]

We were received at the seaside by three other Indians and about twelve or fourteen women and children, who had been there waiting our arrival. Having landed from the canoe, we were conducted by these last to their habitation in the wood, which consisted of three huts or wigwams, there being that number of families amongst them: meanwhile the same two Indians as had brought us went back in their canoe for the three remaining men of our party. On arriving at the hut, we were treated with the greatest humanity by these people; they gave us some broth to sup, but would not suffer us to eat meat, or any kind of substantial food whatever.

The two Indians being come back with our companions, and having all received a tolerable refreshment, I was desired, at the request of a very old woman who appeared to be mistress or mother of the families present, to give them an account of our transactions since the day of our shipwreck. I accordingly gave a more particular account than I had done before in French to the Indian whom I have already mentioned; and he explainedit in his own language to the other Indians. In the course of my relation I could perceive that the old woman was exceedingly affected at certain parts of it; which gave me much satisfaction, as I thence derived hopes that they would continue to treat us with the same humanity. As soon as I had done speaking, the old woman rose up, and after supplying us with some more broth, desired the interpreter to explain to us the shipwreck of the famous French partisan St. Luc Lacorne[19] on his passage from Canada to France.

He informed me that this gentleman, of whose shipwreck I had already heard something, was cast away directly upon the North Cape; that a great number of persons perished on the occasion, amongst whom were two of Mr. St. Luc's children, who were drowned in his arms as he was attempting to carry them on shore. He likewise informed me that, after his having remained five days there, and suffered much from cold and hunger, he himself had relieved him, and conducted him to Louisbourg; for which service, he said, Mr. St. Luc was indebted to him thirty pounds, which he promised to remit from Halifax , but had never performed it. Whether this part of the Indian's story be true or not, it is impossible for me to determine: the gentleman himself is the best acquainted with it.[33] But this I am certain of, that the poor Indians must have earned the money very dearly, in conducting him so far at the season of the year in which the journey was performed.

These people did everything in their power to reduce the swelling from our limbs; which they at length accomplished after much difficulty. Having provided for our own immediate wants, our thoughts recurred to those unfortunate men whom we had left by the wreck. We were under much anxiety for them, lest by this time they might have perished with hunger. However, in case they should be still alive, I was determined no means should be omitted for their preservation; and having described to the Indians the part of the island we were cast away upon, asked them if it was possible to go to their relief?

From the description I gave the Indians of the situation of the river, and of a small island that lay nearly opposite, they said that they knew the place perfectly well; that it was above one hundred miles distant, through very difficult paths, over rivers and mountains; and that, if they undertook the journey, they must expect some compensation for their trouble. This indeed was but reasonable: for it could not be expected that the Indians should leave their hunting, by which alone they subsisted their wives and families, to undergo a fatigue of that kind through pure benevolence: and as to their account of the distance, I could easily give credit to it, as I knew we had come above 150 miles by water. (*This is a conservative estimate. Without allowing for deviations from course, the distance is about one hundred and forty miles.*)

I then informed them for the first time, for in fact it did not occur to me before, that I had some money, and that, if it would be any object to them, I would pay them for their trouble. They seemed much pleased when I told them that I had money, and desired me to let them look at it. Then taking the purse from my servant, I showed them the hundred and eighty guineas that it contained; and observing an eagerness in their countenances at the sight of the coin, which I had little expected amongst Indians; and that the women in particular seemed to have taken a strong fancy to it, I presented them with a guinea each; for which they expressed their satisfaction by laughing,the only method among the savages of displaying every sentiment of that nature.

However I was determined at all events to save the people if any of them remained alive, though the Indians should be ever so exorbitant in their demands; and [I] made an agreement with them at last, that they should set off the next day, which was the second of March, and that they should receive twenty-five guineas at their departure, and the same sum on their return. This being adjusted, they immediately went to work in making a proper number of mawkisins and snow-shoes for themselves and for the men; and three of them went off the next morning, having received the sum of money agreed for.

After these people knew that I had money, my situation amongst them was not near so comfortable as before: for they became as mercenary as they had hitherto been charitable, and exacted above ten times the value for every little necessary they furnished for myself and the rest of my companions. Besides which, I was under constant apprehension lest they should be incited by this extraordinary passion for money to plunder us, and leave us in the same destitute condition in which they found us. The only circumstance on which I founded my hope of better treatment from them was their religion: for, as I mentioned before, they were Christians, and rigid Catholics, having been converted by the French before we got possession of the island. But perhaps it was this very circumstance of their communications with Christians that had inspired them with that vehement love of money.

They showed indeed every mark of attachment to their faith, being very assiduous at their devotions both night and morning; and frequently gave us cause to wish they had not been quite so devout, by disturbing us with their psalm-singing the whole night. I was very much afraid at times, if they had learnt that tenet of their sect of keeping no faith with heretics, that their profession of Christianity would be of little service to us. My servant being an Irish Catholic, they were exceedingly fond of him and heaped their favours upon him very profusely. He joined them for the most part in their roaring, for I cannot with propriety call it singing, and in their prayers; though he did not understand a word of either. Indeed I question much whether they themselves understood them, for they were the most confused jargon I ever heard, compounded of their own and the French language with the mixture of a few broken Latin phrases, which they had picked up from their converters, the Jesuits.

These insular savages bore in general an exact resemblance in their persons and manners to those on the continent of America. The principal points in which they differed were, in having their hair long, which is peculiar to the women alone among the continental Indians, and in wearing caps and breeches. Their language was very different from that of those nations or tribes which I was acquainted with; though I doubt not but it might have been a resemblance to some others upon the continent. I found afterwards, when we got into a part of the island where it was to be had, that they had the same strong propensity to spiritous liquor, so universal among the Indians.

It was some time before we had recovered any degree of strength or could digest any substantial food. The only kind we could get from the Indians was the flesh of moose-deer, and seal oil; on which they subsist entirely during the time of hunting. Notwithstanding that we found ourselves, after our late miseries, pretty comfortably situated amongst those savages, yet I was anxious to get away on account of the dispatches I was charged with, which I thought might be of the utmost consequence to his majesty's service; particularly, as I knew that the duplicates were lost. I continued however in so weak a condition that it was impossible for me to move for some time; and found, as well as my fellow sufferers, that such a shock to the constitution was not easily to be repaired.

After being absent near a fortnight, the Indians arrived with three men, who were the only survivors of the eight who had been left behind at the hut. They were in a very reduced and miserable condition, and informed me, on enquiring the particulars of their transactions from the time we left them, that after having consumed all the beef, they lived for some days on the skin of the moose-deer, which we had left entire, not thinking it worthwhile to make a partition of it. This being consumed, three of them died in a few days of hunger, and the others were under the necessity of subsisting on the flesh of the dead men, till they were relieved by the Indians. One of the remaining five was so imprudently ravenous, when the Indians came to their assistance, as to eat such a quantity of meat that he expired in a few hours, in the greatest agonies imaginable; and another soon after shot himself accidentally with one of the Indian's guns. Thus was our number, which originally consisted of nineteen persons, reduced to nine; and I rather wonder how so many persons could, for the space of three months, go through such complicated distresses, from excessive cold, fatigue, and hunger.

We all remained another fortnight[20] among the Indians, during which I was obliged to pay, as before, a most exorbitant price for our diet, and for every necessary that we were provided with. By this time my health being somewhat re-established, and my money at the same time very much reduced, I was resolved to postpone my own convenience to the good of the service, and to proceed as fast as possible with General Haldimand's dispatches, though it was now the most unfavourable season of the year for travelling. I therefore made an agreement with the Indians to conduct me to Halifax; for which I was to pay them forty-five pounds, and to furnish them with provisions and all necessaries at every inhabited place on our way.

IT WAS SETTLED THAT I SHOULD depart on the 2nd of April, with two Indians for Halifax, accompanied by Mr. Winslow, a young gentleman who had been a passenger on board the vessel and was one of the three survivors at the hut, together with my own servant. The Indians were to conduct the remainder of our party to a settlement on Spanish River (*Sydney Harbour*), about fifty miles distant (*actually, a scant thirty miles*), where they were to remain till the spring, when an opportunity might offer for them to get by sea to Halifax. Previously to parting I gave the captain cash for a bill on his owner at New York, to provide for the immediate subsistence of himself and the sailors; which bill was afterwards protested by the owner, on the pretence that the ship being lost, neither master nor crew were entitled to any wages.

We accordingly set off on the day appointed, each carrying four pairs of Indian shoes, or mawkisins, a pair of snow-shoes, and provisions for fifteen days. The same day we got to a place called by the English Broad Oar (*Bras d'Or*),[21] where we were detained the following day by a snow storm. On the 4th we again proceeded through the woods about five leagues; and on the 5th arrived at a place named Broad Deck (*Baddeck*),[22] which lies at the entrance of a very fine salt-water lake, called Lake St. Peter. This lake communicates by a narrow inlet with the sea, from which it is distant about sixteen leagues. At this place we met with two families of Indians who were hunting there, and purchased of them a bark canoe for five pounds; the Indians having informed me that some parts of the great lake are never frozen, and that it was requisite to have a canoe to pass over those places; and as we were to travel over the ice in other parts of it, I was obliged to purchase two sleighs, in which we were to place the canoe and drag it after us.

Having remained two days in this place and provided ourselves with a few other necessary articles, we proceeded on the 7th for a few miles along the lake;[23] but the ice being bad, we were soon obliged to take to the woods. A thaw coming on soon after, with rain, made the snow, which lay to the depth of six feet in the woods, so soft and heavy that we could travel no longer on snow-shoes, the snow sticking to them in large quantities. We were therefore obliged to make a fire and remain here; and the thaw continuing for the space of four days made us very apprehensive lest the ice should give way altogether; for the spring was now too far advanced to travel any longer on the snow, unless during a frost. We should then have been under the necessity of waiting till the ice was entirely cleared off the lake; which would have taken at least a fortnight or three weeks from the time of its breaking up; in which case we might have been reduced to a condition equally distressed with that we had been in after our shipwreck, except that we were [now] provided with arms and ammunition.

However the frost returned on the 12th, and the next day we set off and travelled about six leagues, sometimes on floating pieces of ice, and at others in our canoe, where the lake was open. On the 14th, our provisions being nearly exhausted, I proposed going in search of some game, as the country abounded with deer; for the Indians in general never think of providing for the next day's wants, but eat on without reflection whilst they have a morsel of food remaining. I accordingly went with one of the Indians into the woods. We had not been three hours on the hunt before we discovered a very fine moose-deer; and the Indian shot him in about an hour after. We skinned this animal, which weighed about six hundred pounds, loaded ourselves with some of the best parts of its flesh as well as the blood, which the Indian took care to collect, putting it in the bladder of the beast; and returned to our canoe. We then sent the other Indian, Mr. Winslow, and my servant, for some more of the meat, of which they brought about an hundred pounds.

Being now well stocked with provisions, we had no reason to apprehend that we should want in case a return of mild weather should render it impossible for us to travel either upon the lake or in the woods. On the 15th we set out very early in the morning, and pursued our journey about six leagues in the same manner as before. The greatest inconvenience that we felt was the want of bread, which the Indians of this country never make use of whilst they are hunting; and being now much wearied with travelling, our strength having been greatly exhausted by our past fatigues, we agreed to make a halt for a day or two in the woods.

What renders the travelling through the woods in these cold climates more tolerable than might be supposed during the winter season, is the number of pine trees and other evergreens which are interspersed in different parts; the branches of which serve, not only to lie upon, but also as a shelter from the severity of the weather. We chose a spot abounding with these trees, and it is almost inconceivable in how short a time the Indians made us a comfortable habitation of the boughs, called in their language a wigwam.

Their method of constructing them is as follows: having chosen the spot for their fire, they first clear off the snow, throwing it into a bank in a circular form, leaving a vacant space, or passage, to leeward: and it is to be observed that the more snow there is on the ground the better, as it makes the best part of the shelter. They then cut branches of pine of a proper length, and placing the thicker ends of them in the bank of snow, bend and interweave them towards the top. These branches are crossed by others, and interwoven with smaller ones, in such a manner as to afford a sufficient shelter from the wind and from the falling snow. The fire is made in the middle of the wigwam, and the smoke of it goes out by the passage to leeward. The wigwams thus made are very comfortable, even in the coldest weather, and are proof against anything but a heavy rain; besides which, a change of wind is the only inconvenience they are liable to.

WE PROCEEDED AGAIN on our journey on the 18th, and, during that and the following day, travelled several miles without meeting with anything remarkable. I had now leisure to observe the beauties of this lake, which was one of the finest I ever saw in America; though at this season of the year it could not appear to the best advantage. As far as I could judge, it is about twenty leagues in length from north to south, and eight wide from east to west.[24] A number of small islands are scattered about in different parts of it, and gives it somewhat the appearance of the lake of Killarny [sic], and other fresh-water lakes in Ireland. These islands have never been settled on; yet appear to be very fruitful, and must be a most delightful residence in summer except for the want of fresh water; which perhaps may be the reason they have never been inhabited. Had the lake been properly frozen, we might have saved ourselves the trouble of travelling several leagues by crossing over from point to point, and from one island to another; but, this not being the case, we were obliged to travel round the greatest part of the bays on one side of it.[25]

On the 20th we arrived at a place called St. Peter's where there are four or five French and English families settled. I was here received very politely and entertained at the house of a Mr. Cavanaught (*Lawrence Kavanagh*),[26] a merchant, who was so good as to take my draught for 200 pounds upon my father, though I was a perfect stranger to him. To this harbour vessels of the greatest burthen can come with safety, and a considerable fishery was formerly carried on here, till on the breaking out of the present war, the American privateers put a stop to it.

The force of these privateers, even taken collectively, is but trifling; and it is much to be regretted that government cannot spare a vessel or two of the force to cruize about here, and protect the fisheries; which, together with some other branches of trade, might be carried on with as much vigour and much more benefit than before the war. This Mr. Cavanaught, but a short time before I arrived, was plundered to the amount of three thousand pounds by two privateers from Boston; who came in at their leisure and took what they wanted out of his stores. These American privateers have likewise driven all the settlers away from Louisbourg, who had also subsisted by the fishery; and it is somewhat remarkable that this place which was, during the last two wars, such a bone of contention between us and the French, has not at the present moment so much as a single inhabitant.

I should have taken a shallop or fishing-boat from this place and gone to Halifax by sea, but that there was almost a certainty of being taken by some privateer along the coast. This lake St. Peter is but half a mile from the ocean, to which we were to carry our canoe through the woods, and to proceed by water to the Gut of Canceau. While the French were in possession of the island, they had formed a design of cutting through this narrow neck of land, and opening a communication on that side between the ocean and the lake, in order to bring in their large ships of war to lie during the winter in the lake of St. Peter; for there is a sufficient depth of water in the harbour of St. Peter for the largest ships of the line to ride, though there is not water enough in the inlet by which the lake communicates with the ocean to enable them to pass up to the harbour.

After stocking ourselves with as much provisions and other necessaries as we had occasion for, we set off on the 22nd in our bark canoe, and arrived the same day at a place called by the French, Grand Grave (*Grand Greve*);[27] where there is a family or two of that nation. The wind blowing hard, we were obliged to remain here all night, and on the 23rd proceeded along the coast to a settlement called Discousse, where we were detained another day by some floating ice.

On the 25th we got to a place Narrashoc (*Arichat*);[28] where we were as hospitably entertained as we had been at St. Peter's. I here exchanged the remains of my regimental coat for a brown suit of cloaths, intending to pass for the master of the ship in case I should happen to be taken by any of the American privateers at Canceau; and as the inhabitants of this place gave me to understand that the people of Canceau were very much disaffected to government, I took every precaution to disguise the appearance of an officer.

We proceeded in our canoe, on the 26th, to the point of Isle Madame;[29] intending to cross the great passage of Canceau. This passage is called the Gut of Canceau, from an Acadian settlement of that name on the continent; and separates the Island of Cape Breton from Acadia, or, as it is now called by the English, Nova Scotia. The island of Madame lies in the middle of the gut, but rather nearer to Cape Breton than to the main; and the passage to this island is called the Small, that from the Island to Canceau, the Great Passage. On making the point of Isle Madame, we found that there was still a great quantity of floating ice in the Great Passage, and, not thinking it prudent to venture in our frail vessel amongst it, we returned to Narrashoc in order to procure a small sloop or vessel that could resist the ice.

Having accordingly provided one, we embarked our little canoe in it, and, on the 27th, the wind being as favourable as we could wish, got across the passage, which is eight leagues, in three hours. (*Prenties' estimate of twenty miles is some eight miles too great.*) The men who navigated the vessel to the other side were very apprehensive of some American privateers lying in the harbour of Canceau,[30] having seen several in the bay two days before. Upon this intelligence, I gave my dispatches and papers to one of the Indians, knowing well that they never attempt to search or plunder any of these people. We were however so fortunate as to see no privateers on entering the harbour.

ON LANDING AT CANCEAU, I went to the house of Mr. Rust, who is the principal man at this place and acts as justice of the peace under government, for which he receives about £100 per annum. The inhabitants on the other side, as well as the people who brought us over, having informed me that this gentleman always supplied the New England cruizers with every necessary that his stores could afford, I was determined to be very cautious in everything I said in his presence.

Having paid the person who brought us over the gut and thanked him for his private intelligence, I was conducted to the house of this Mr. Rust, to whom I passed myself for the captain of the ship. He asked me a number of questions, the tendency of which I could easily perceive; and [I] therefore gave him as evasive answers as possible. I found that he had a brother-in-law who was a first lieutenant on board a sixteen-gun brig belonging to Boston, which had gone out of the harbour of Canceau the day before.

We remained in this place till three o'clock the next morning, when, being apprehensive of treachery on the part of our pretended friends, we set off without any intimation of it to Mr. Rust. From this gentleman I had purchased a piece of salt pork and about eight pounds of biscuit, which he said was as much as he could spare and for which I was obliged to pay him at least thrice its value. We were now to proceed in our canoe along the coast to Halifax, and had reason to fear that we should be again distressed for provisions. However, we were so lucky as to find, as we coasted along, plenty of lobsters and other fish, which the Indians caught with prodigious dexterity, killing the flat fish with a pointed pole, and the lobsters with a cloven one. We were ten days going from Canceau to Halifax, during which interval we did not meet with any settlement, and saw nothing worth mentioning, except a number of piccaroons on various parts of the coast.

The Indians remained for a few days at Halifax ; when, having received the balance due to them, they took their departure for the island. I was obliged to continue here for two months longer, till an opportunity served of a passage in the Royal Oak, to New York; where I delivered my dispatches (in a very ragged condition) to Sir Henry Clinton.

The rest of my fellow sufferers in the shipwreck soon after arrived at Halifax in a shallop from Spanish River. The captain, conscious of the reception he would meet with, did not think proper to go to his owner at New York to give an account of the loss of his vessel; but took his passage in a ship from Halifax to London, and now serves as a pilot on the Thames. The mate was, on account of his good conduct during the whole of our transactions, appointed by a gentleman in Halifax to the command of a ship bound to the West Indies.

THE END of Ensign Prenties' *Narrative*

EPILOGUE by G. G. Campbell

ENSIGN PRENTIES ARRIVED in Halifax on or about May eighth, 1781. Nine weeks later he got round to writing a report on his experiences for transmission to Governor Haldimand, who received it on the second of November, almost a year after Prenties' departure from Quebec. The report is a concise account of the events which Prenties was later to describe in detail in his *Narrative*. In one place only do the two accounts diverge. The weeks-long period of recuperation that followed his rescue by the Indians Prenties actually spent in an army outpost on Sydney Harbour, not in the Indian encampment on St. Ann's Bay. The pertinent section of the report reads as follows:

"After we had recovered and recruited our strength a little, I agreed with the Indians to conduct us to Spanish River, being the first settlement, and was obliged to pay them before they set out Forty Pounds. After I got there, Captn. Thomas Green who commanded at this place treated myself and the rest of the people with the greatest humanity. He informed me he expected Your Excellency would send a vessel from Quebec this summer for coals. I remained at Spanish River a few weeks to recover my health. And as Your Excellency's despatches were of some consequence, I hired two Indians at a very great price and travelled from there to this place [Halifax] in twenty-two days, where I have remained untill this time waiting for a vessel bound for [New] York, and am to go tomorrow in His Majesty's ship *Royal Oak*....."[31]

It is not strange that Prenties should have gone at the first opportunity from the squalor and restricted diet of the Indian encampment to the comforts of an army outpost. He was canny enough to sense, however, that the sophisticated audience he hoped to reach with his little book would relish the picture of distressed Britishers cared for by savage Indians. Army outposts were well enough known, in all conscience, but Rousseau's noble savage, in all his pristine virtue, was everywhere an object of interest and curiosity—except to those who had encountered him in the flesh. So Prenties, mindful of his audience—as ever the teller-of-tales must be—did as was done by every storm-tossed, fate-driven wanderer since Odysseus: he improved the locale.

Prenties delivered his dispatches to Sir Henry Clinton's New York headquarters on August nineteenth. Since they had been nine months in transit, they could not have been received with much interest, even if staff officers had not had before them a problem of some urgency.

For many months the war in the New York theatre had been a stalemate. American forces and their French allies ringed the city and its port in a giant semicircle. But just before Prenties' arrival Clinton had become aware that General George Washington was making changes in the disposition of his forces. Clinton, naturally, took these movements to mean that an attack was to be made on some point in his defences; the question was where to expect it. Actually, Clinton had been hoodwinked; Washington was planning no attack on New York. Instead, he was in great secrecy withdrawing the bulk of his forces for a swift movement to the south where Lord Cornwallis, with an army of seventy-five hundred men, was penned up in Yorktown. A French navy was on the way up from the West Indies, and Washington planned, in a joint operation of the two services, to force Cornwallis to capitulate. So it was that, when Clinton awoke to what was happening, Britain's last hope of preserving intact her American dominions was being extinguished at Yorktown. Cornwallis surrendered on October nineteenth.

It is not to be wondered, matters being what they were in New York, that Ensign Prenties came and went almost unnoticed. He did have an interview with Lord Dalrymple, Clinton's aide-de-camp, who gave a sympathetic hearing to his tale of suffering and loss, advising him to make a claim for recompense in London. So before the year was out Prenties crossed the Atlantic to seek reparation for his losses. To justify his claims, he prepared for government officials a detailed report of his misadventure. This report, dressed up and expanded for publication, was soon on sale in London bookshops.

Prenties did amazingly well for himself. An unknown colonial of humble rank, he not only had his claims allowed by government, he established himself as an author as well. Almost certainly he had influential patrons working on his behalf. Two who might have helped him were resident in London. Sir James Murray, Canada's first British governor, was one of these: years before, on being recalled from Canada, Murray had left his household slaves in the keeping of Prenties' father. The other was Sir Guy Carleton, Colonel of the 84th Regiment, whose interest in Canadian affairs had never waned, and whose advice on Canada was often sought by the king's ministers. One or both of these men might have given Prenties a helping hand.

Helping hand or not, Prenties had a modest success with his little book. Before he left for Canada in May, 1782, the first edition had been run through and a second was in preparation. In all, the book was to run to five editions. Two years after it first appeared an artist called Smirke, at work on a series of paintings to illustrate marine disasters, chose Prenties' experience as a subject for the eleventh painting in the series. Of this painting an engraving was made for the printer's use.[32] Entitled "The Departure," it depicts Prenties and his five companions as they set off from Margaree Harbour in their search for help. While it is not remarkable for artistic merit, its very existence testifies to the interest aroused in London by Prenties' *Narrative*.

London reviewers took note of the little book, and ran the gamut from forthright condemnation to modified eulogy. *The London Review* was admirably succinct and pointed:

"This narrative contains little that can amuse any reader. The incidents are told with coldness. The author can neither instruct nor please. The matter is often vulgar, sometimes silly and always insipid. The performance will be opened without anxiety, and thrown aside with disgust."[33]

The European Magazine was hardly more kind; and its reviewer used the opportunity to lament, in Gibbonian periods, that ordinary people like Prenties should be tempted into writing books, a business best left to professionals like himself; that is to say, to those who could write Gibbonian prose.[34] *The Monthly Review* gave an extended notice containing observations that are patently true.

"The resources to avoid cold, and sustain life, amidst this scene of wretchedness, almost realize the fiction of DeFoe in his *Robinson Crusoe*; and probably exceed the contrivances of Alexander Selkirk, the genuine hero of that admired story. The present narrative is very interesting. It is related with moderation and good sense. The author hath given us a striking example of unshaken fortitude; and at the same time hath displayed a fertility of invention, more particularly conspicuous in the most desperate situations...."[35]

It is unlikely Prenties ever read the reviews, for by May, 1782, he was on his way back to Canada. He had purchased a lieutenancy in the 84th Regiment and now travelled in style, and in distinguished company. On board were many civil and military dignitaries, including the Honourable Henry Hamilton, newly appointed Lieutenant-Governor of Canada, and Brigadier-General Allan MacLean, Officer Commanding the 84th. The war, now entering its seventh year, had brought little honour to British arms. So General MacLean and Lieutenant Prenties could look back with some pride to the night of fighting in which both had shared and which had saved Quebec from the Revolution. The convoy in which they sailed reached Quebec on June twenty-third.

In August Lieutenant Prenties was back with his regiment, apparently at St. Jean. His subsequent military career can be briefly sketched. Before the month was out Prenties was under arrest in Montreal for "ungentleman like behaviour." During the fall and winter, while correspondence concerning him went back and forth between Quebec and Montreal, he remained under arrest. Not until June was he reinstated in his commission.

Two months after his resuming duty, detachments of the 84th moved to western outposts on board the *Seneca*, a vessel plying between Carleton Island and Niagara. On August seventeenth, at Niagara, what was described as a "riot" broke out on the *Seneca*. Lieutenant Prenties was arrested as one of those involved. A report on the affair went all the way to Quebec, and Haldimand ordered a court martial. The court martial, held at Niagara, found Prenties guilty as charged but recommended clemency, pointing out that, while the rigour of military law allowed no other verdict, there were sound reasons why Prenties should be treated with leniency and humanity. While the findings of the court martial[36] went back to Quebec for review by the Commander-in-Chief, Prenties remained under arrest at Niagara.

Apparently he was allowed much freedom, for the Officer Commanding gave him permission to go with two friends to visit the fort at Oswego, distant some days' sail from Niagara. So Lieutenant Prenties, Lieutenant Graham and a certain David Smith, accompanied by their servants, set off in a small vessel, a light-hearted and convivial company. After three days at Oswego, Prenties and Graham went on to Carleton Island, where Prenties got the good news that he had again been reinstated in his command.

A few days later, however, ten of the regimental officers on duty at Carleton Island notified the Officer Commanding that they could no longer serve with Lieutenants Graham and Prenties, since these young men had engaged in conduct not becoming to gentlemen. The two were placed under arrest, and a court of inquiry convened.

To read the records of the inquiry[37] is to observe a tempest in a teapot. David Smith, the same one who had gone to Oswego, had recently been court-martialed and dismissed the service. In ceasing to be an officer he had ceased also to be a gentleman. Prenties and Graham, by intimate association with one who was no longer a gentleman, had demeaned themselves and disgraced the regiment. There was no denying the evidence: the two were guilty as charged. Prenties was given the choice of selling his commission or of standing trial at court martial. He was ordered to Quebec, there to await the pleasure of the Commander-in-Chief. So as the year 1783 drew to a close, he was back home in the House of the Golden Dog, addressing a letter of contrition and appeal to Sir Richard Haldimand.[38]

In the meantime, the war had dragged to an end, the terms of the peace had been agreed upon, and Haldimand had instructions from London to disband the 84th Regiment. A career officer who had given long years of distinguished service in British America, Haldimand looked with bitterness on the inglorious end to a badly managed war, a war that many believed would never have come about but for the bungling of politicians at Westminster. Compared to the failure of those in high places, the peccadillos of a fractious junior officer seemed now of small consequence. Lieutenant Prenties was restored to his commission, entitling him to retirement on half-pay for the rest of his natural life.

THE OFFICERS AND MEN of the 84th scattered far, most of them to take up the land grants to which their military service entitled them. Some went to Nova Scotia, some to Gaspesia, many to the country about Cataraqui, now Kingston. Walter Prenties and his brother John established themselves in a fishing business in Gaspesia. In 1785, on behalf of himself and his two sons, Miles Prenties petitioned for a large grant of land in the area between Gaspé and Percé.[39] No action seems to have been taken on the petition, but the two young men continued for some years to operate their business in that area.

In one way John Prenties' army career ran parallel to that of his brother Walter. He advanced quickly to the rank of ensign, then to that of lieutenant, thanks, no doubt, to Miles Prenties' generosity in providing for his sons.[40] John's career, however, evinced nothing like the propensity for trouble that was evident in Walter. John Thomas wrote no memorials to the high command, found no mention in military correspondence, was summonsed to no courts martial, did not visit Cape Breton. Mute and undistinguished, he did his seven years of military service and then, like Walter, was retired on half-pay.

The brothers carried on their business in Gaspesia until 1790.[41] In that year they moved to a more suitable location on Miramichi Bay. There, on Bay du Vin Island (*the Prenties brothers wrote the name as* Beduin Island), they built a substantial dwelling house, storehouses and a variety of other structures required in their business. They employed a number of indentured fishermen, and engaged the services of other settled in the vicinity. In 1794 they secured the sum of twelve hundred pounds by mortgaging their island to a London businessman. With this new capital they set about to expand and diversify their activities. They acquired land on Bay du Vin River with the intention of raising cattle, and on the river itself they set about to construct a watermill for sawing lumber: a spring freshet swept away the half-constructed mill, and this project was abandoned.[42]

While their sons were busy about their affairs in Gaspesia and Miramichi, Miles and Elizabeth Prenties remained in Quebec. Miles died in 1787, and the House of the Golden Dog was sold to the Freemasons of Quebec, thereafter to be known as Freemasons' Hall. In her declining years Elizabeth went to live with Fanny Thompson, her niece. On Christmas Day, 1799, she made her will. Three days later she died and was buried beside her husband in the English Cathedral. She was sixty-four.

In dictating her Last Will and Testament, Elizabeth made a curious mistake; she bequeathed the bulk of her property to "my son John Walter Prenties": curious, because her only surviving son was John Thomas Prenties. Sometime earlier in that year of 1799, Samuel Walter had sickened and died at his home on Bay du Vin Island.[43] He was buried there, and John Thomas left the island never to return. There is no evidence that either of the brothers ever married or left descendants.

END of the EPILOGUE to Ensign Prenties' *Narrative*

Samuel Burrows' *Narrative*

OF THE

LOSS

OF THE SHIP *WYTON*

ON THE

ISLAND OF CAPE BRETON

AND OF THE

SUFFERINGS OF THE CREW

1823

Advertisement to Samuel Burrows

The following *Narrative* is written by a Seaman, who has four times been shipwrecked, has four times returned to his family pennyless and distressed, but till this last, this fatal disaster, with a body as unbroken as his spirit. He has so artlessly described his sufferings and those of his comrades, that he has been advised to publish his *Narrative* in its original form. It needs no comment, no illustrations; and the heart that cannot feel for the sufferings it describes, is not worthy to be excited by a more highly wrought drama. The facts speak for themselves, and we have not a doubt that they will reach the hearts of his benevolent townsmen.

Since the following *Narrative* went to the press, Samuel Burrows, Edward Taylor, and John Simpson, have each had a leg amputated. The two former were operated on in the Infirmary, where they still remain doing well; the latter lies in his own house, and is fast recovering from the operation.

Hull, 29th March, 1825.

Samuel Burrows' *Narrative*

SEPTEMBER THE 9th, in the year of our Lord, 1823, the ship *Wyton*, Capt. Richard Collinson, left the river Humber, bound on a voyage to Mirimichi. On Wednesday, Thursday and Friday following, the wind was from the northward, and Capt. Collinson thought of bearing up to go south about. On Saturday the 13th, at five a.m. got a fresh breeze from the S.S.W. Flamborough a-head; bore S.W. by S. distance seven or eight miles. The 14th, strong breezes; steering sails set low and aloft. The 15th, at six a.m. saw the island of Covinsha; at two p.m. North Randalsha light-house. Bore S. W. strong breezes: took in top-gallant sails, first reef of the top sails. Nothing particular occurred except strong gales from the westward, sometimes under close reefed topsails and reefed foresail, till about the 28th or 29th of September, when Capt. Collinson spoke the *John Hasdale*, of London, in longitude 38.48. (the latitude slipt my memory) bound for Hull as he said. Captain Collinson desired him, on his arrival, to report us. On the 17th (*October*), light airs and varying, with slight breezes. We here fell in with the *Royalist* of Liverpool, bound to Mirimichi, we lowered the boat down, and Mr. Collinson went on board. Shortly after, he returned on board the *Wyton*, and we got a fresh breeze from the westward.

On the 19th, the wind came from the southward; we made all possible sail. Thursday the 23rd, at four a.m. made Cape North (*Cape Breton Island*), close in with the broken water. The wind shifting from the westward of the land, this circumstance was much in our favour. We made sail and stood to the northward. At eleven, we spoke a brig from Richibucto; she belonged to Shields, and was bound to Hull. Mr. Collinson requested the captain to report us.

At two p.m. St. Paul's Island bore S.S.E. 1/2 E. distance eight miles, wind west. 24th, we got a light breeze from the S.E.; set steering sail. 25th, light breezes and fine weather. We saw something off the weather bow we at first took to be a wreck, but soon made it out to be a dead fish. We lowered the boat, and took with us a sword and some cabin knives and went to it, but, from want of proper tools, we could get but little cut from it; it was a large clinker-built finner, full of barnacles. We found a harpoon in him, with some line attached thereto. I succeeded in getting the line, but could not get the harpoon, it being so far under water: we discovered several sharks round him. We returned to the ship, hoisted our boat, and made sail—fresh breezes.

26th, at four a.m. in steering sails; at eight in topgallant sails, reefed the topsails; spoke the *Royalist*; we had strong breezes with sleet. At ten we got a pilot on board, and made sail for the bar of Mirimichi. We passed the *Hope*, of Whitehaven, riding with loss of her rudder and topmasts. Mr. Collinson spoke her; the captain told us he had been ashore. At three p.m. brought up abreast of the ballast quay, and the ship's crew were employed in getting the ship alongside of the ballast quay. Monday the 27th, we were employed heaving ballast and striking top-gallant masts.

Wednesday the 29th, the mate and five more hands went up the river with the skiff for a raft of timber. On the 30th, at four a.m. they returned with the raft; hove the ship from the ballast quay, moored her, and began to take in the cargo.

Nothing particular occurred till Friday, Nov. 14, when an immense quantity of ice came down the river and broke the rafts adrift from the ship, but we were so fortunate as to get them all again. We were completely loaded by Sunday the 16th, and on the 17th and 18th our people were employed in watering the ship, getting the boats in, and returning the spare timber. On Wednesday the 19th, we unmoored the ship, and at six p.m. the pilot and the master came on board: we warped out, but did not get under weigh.

On Thursday the 20th, at six a.m. we had strong breezes from the N.W. We ran the kedge out to take the ship from the shore; we succeeded in getting under weigh, slipt the kedge and towline and the skiff, and four hands with some labourers went to weigh it.

At ten a.m. we brought up off Chatham: I believe the men were employed in bending the mizen and mizen top-sail. Here we took on board Mr. Carmard, Mr. Douglass the stower, Mr. M'Cullum the pilot, with three passengers for Liverpool. We got the skiff on board, weighed anchor, and made sail down the river. We took in tow a boat and four hands belonging to the *General Graham*, the ship running through heavy ice: spoke the *General Graham*; Mr. Collinson and he intended to keep company; the boat left us at meridian. We took the ground on the bar and let go the anchor; the ship fell over it and broke it; we run the kedge out, and succeeded in getting the ship off at five p.m. and brought up in four fathoms water. Our people were employed getting the waste anchor over, &c. The 21st, light breezes but very thick weather. At six a.m. we got the ship under weigh, the boat a-head, sounding at ten ditto in boat: latter part, we had fresh breezes with snow and sleet.

Saturday, Nov. 22.— The latter part of these twenty-four hours we had strong breezes, with constant drifts of snow; sounded at intervals 30 and 35 fathoms; wind N.N.W. At midnight fresh gales; took in main top-gallant sail, and one reef of the topsails; sounded and found 21 fathoms. Capt. Collinson expected the ship to be off the south end of the Magdalen Islands; he made sure of this when the ship deepened her water, as we had 22 and 23 fathoms for several casts. Sunday the 23d, at half-past one a.m. I went down to inform the master it was coming on to blow stronger. He told me to call the people up to double reef the topsails. The carpenter fell out of the fore rigging, and was severely hurt.

At half-past two the gale still increasing, with a constant drift of snow, we called all hands to reef the foresail and close reef the topsails. In hauling up the foresail, the fore-yard broke in two. We were several hours in stowing the headsails, being so frozen. John Simpson lay in the foretop, and could not make any assistance to get down; at length he was lowered down by Mr. Collinson himself, and taken into the cabin. He there had him shifted and put to bed.

Sounded 35 fathoms, the ship labouring and shipping much water, which washed all the bulwark and quarter boards away, and water casks off the decks. At six a.m. set the storm fore staysail and main staysail, and mizen staysail. Shortly after, they all blew to pieces. All hands employed at the pumps, the ship making much water. At eight a.m. 40 fathoms, it still blowing to excess, with heavy falls of snow; at ten 40 fathoms, and at eleven 45 fathoms; Mr. Collinson wore the ship to the westward, and thought, if we went on shore near Cheticamp, we might save our lives, not expecting that we were so far down the Gulf.

The wind still blowing tremendously we thought of cutting the masts away to see if she would ride, but were fearful she would not, as the sea ran so very high.— Sounded and found 40 fathoms, and shortly after 45 fathoms; at five p.m. Mr. Collinson called all hands into the cabin to prayers. Having committed our perilous situation and our lives into the hands of the Almighty, and prayers being over, we close reefed the main topsail balance, and reefed the mizen; a little after eight Mr. Collinson sent word to me to let a reef out of the mizen, and to shackle the chain cable to the rope cable, but at this awful instant land was discovered, and the cry of "Lord have mercy upon us," resounded through the whole ship, and, "for God's sake come up and try to save your lives." We immediately ran with all speed to cut away the anchors, but were unfortunately too late.

At half-past eight p.m. the ship struck. The scene at this tremendous moment was shocking to behold; such a dark dismal snowy night, and a tremendous heavy sea; we were all now driven as it were to our wits' end; some of the crew took to the main rigging, and some to the fore rigging; Mr. Collinson, Mr. M'Cullum the pilot, John Parsons, and myself, took up the mizen rigging, expecting to get off the mizen topsail yard upon the rocks. The ship striking so heavily, she soon listed off, and we came down on the larboard side of the mizen rigging; it was there I had nearly lost the first joint of my middle finger, by the crossjack yard. In coming down I passed the second mate, when he exclaimed, "Lord have mercy upon my poor wife and family."

The captain and I grappled along the side to the fore chains, and there I saw the carpenter and pilot, but I soon lost sight of the carpenter amongst the timber and breakers. Here I remained hanging over the side, below the fore chains, by the chain cable, which was hanging over the side, for about the space of half an hour, but the ship breaking up fast, I hove myself on to the timber, and was washed a-head of the ship once or twice.

At last, with great exertion and hard struggling, I reached the shore, when Mr. Collinson came and took me by the hand to assist me in getting out. Soon after I found six others, viz. James M'Cullum, Thomas Crompton, Edward Taylor, John Simpson, William Webster, who had his leg broke in getting on shore, and the boy Warcup; these were all that reached the shore out of seventeen, of which the crew consisted, and three passengers; all the rest of our companions in tribulation found a watery grave. Mr. Collinson called us all together to take shelter in the creek of a rock, to keep one another warm. Here we remained till the sea began to wash over us. It being very dark, we ascended the rocks into a wood, where we all kept close together, waiting for the dawn of day, and our comfortless situation made us think it would never return.

Towards daylight the boy Warcup kept creeping about our feet, frequently calling Ned, one of our unfortunate men; at length the poor boy turned on his side and died, he being literally frozen to death; we cut fir branches to cover him.

The master and three others went down to the creek, as soon as it was light, to view the wreck, and I soon after followed; there we found the long boat and skiff, the long boat was much stove, and the skiff, having the upper stroke gone, was much shook in the bottom.— The master picked up a small keg of gin belonging to me which held about a gallon; being iron hooped, or bound, it did not break up so soon; also, a small keg of wine, containing about a gallon. We saw with great regret the dead bodies of several of our shipmates; unfortunately we could find no provisions, not so much as a single biscuit. I observed to the captain that it was a fortunate circumstance that we had the boat, so that we might have a prospect of saving our lives when the weather became fine and calm, but it still continued to blow very hard, with constant drifts of snow.

The ship was now entirely broken up and dashed to pieces; we went to the bush, and found the two pigs which we had with us in the boats; we caught one of them, which the master killed, but the other ran into the wood. We now tried all possible means to get a light, but to no effect, every thing about us being so damp and wet. It was thought by the master and Mr. M'Cullum, the pilot, who was a resident of that country, to be the most advisable thing for us to travel to the westward, towards Cheticamp, which they supposed was not above twenty miles distance. Each of us took a piece of the pork on our backs, the master the small keg of gin, and the pilot the wine; those were all the provisions we had to subsist on.

Monday, Nov. 24.— We commenced travelling in search of houses. We were under the painful necessity of leaving the cook, who unfortunately had his leg broke, and in a very bad state, behind us; we heard his heart-rending cries for a long time, and it was our intention, if we were so fortunate as to find a house, to send for him as soon as possible. In travelling on, we passed several trees that had been burnt, which gave us great heartening to go forward. We came to several high mountains, which we found very difficult to get up, being so close to the sea, and some of them nearly perpendicular, so that we had to pull ourselves up by the trees; I not being able to get on so well as my brother sufferers, was persuaded by the pilot to leave my leather jacket behind me. He being the best on foot, always kept the lead, and picked out the best road for us.

Night making its approach, we cut down branches of the trees to lie down on. We took a little of our raw pork, and each of us took a drink out of the kegs of wine and gin with our mouths, not having any thing else to drink out of. It still continuing to snow and blow very hard, I kept walking about all the night to keep my feet from freezing, and I sometimes fell down by the side of a tree, overpowered with sleep as I walked. Through the course of a long dreary night we took a little spirits; each bemoaning his hard fate. The pilot came and walked by me, when he persuaded me to lie down a little while, and I found myself very stiff when we got up.

Tuseday, Nov. 25.— Partaking of some raw pork and a little of the spirits, we began to travel up the mountains. Having to pull ourselves through the trees and bushes, we suffered for want of mittens: only Mr. Collinson had a pair of gloves amongst all our company. I cut part of the comfortable, which was round my neck, to wrap my hands in; others took pieces of their handkerchiefs, or pieces of old cloth. We saw no wild beasts, but discovered several of their foot marks, and scarce a bird was to be seen on the island.

Towards meridian we had light airs and fine weather; we directed our course down by the sea shore. We saw two ships becalmed and haul down to the northward, which made us all regret having left the wreck, as we knew there was no possible means of attracting their notice where we were situated, though we kept our eyes anxiously fixed upon them for a considerable time, supposing we might not live to see another ship pass that way; in short, such was our fatigue and absolute distress, that the meanest Indian hut was all I prayed for. We were obliged to go farther up the mountains, as there was no possibility of getting along the sea shore. We partook of a little of the raw pork, our wine and spirits being quite exhausted, but we always found plenty of water.— My feet now began to swell prodigiously, so that I was obliged to cut my boots open to ease them.

In the course of our travels we came to a large fall of water from the mountains, which they all crossed before me, in attempting which I slipt, and my hat fell into the stream, and I should scarcely have been able to have got it out, but for the kind assistance of Thomas Crompton, who got it out for me. Soon after this I found the blood coming through my stockings, occasioned by the intense frost; I also saw the blood streaming from the feet of Edward Taylor, and one of his toes turned very black.— John Simpson's shoes were nearly worn off his feet, and in a very bad state. The master, Mr. Collinson, had on a pair of half boots, and it was with sorrow I observed that his pantaloons were much torn, and his knees scratched with making his way through the bushes; yet, in the midst of all this complicated distress, I never heard him complain. Thomas Crompton had a pair of new boots, which I think were the means of saving his feet; the pilot had a pair of half boots with cloth tops, but he was in all respects the best at travelling of our whole company.

We made down to the water side to see if we could discover the low land of Cheticamp, but there was none to be seen, nor could we discover the smallest prospect of finding a house to put our heads in. Shortly after, it was thought by Mr. M'Cullum to be the most advisable method to return back, which was now agreed to; still the master,

Mr. Collinson, thought it was best to go forward, but at length we all agreed, and turned back. We had not travelled far, however, before Mr. Collinson said to me, "Mr. Burrows, I am persuaded we are doing very wrong in turning back, I am sure we cannot be far from the houses now." I with him was of opinion, that as we had got so far it was the best to go forward; as such, we turned ourselves about again, and travelled forward.

We came to a run of water, and here we stopped and partook of the pork, but our company not being able to eat it, in consequence of being so faint, we kept a little of it in our mouths, and this served to keep us from drinking so much cold water. All our small stock of wine and spirits being done, we were sore grieved, and I prayed earnestly to the Lord, in his great mercy, to conduct us to a house, or we soon must perish.

We travelled on, but not the least prospect of finding one, and night coming on fast, we began to look for a place to rest in for the night, where the best shelter was to be found from the trees. We cut down the branches to lie on; it being so very cold, and so much snow falling from the trees upon us, made us tremble excessively, and shake all the night long, and earnestly pray to the Lord for the morning light. It was during this night more especially I found the want of my leather jacket, which caused me to regret much having been persuaded to leave it behind me.

Wednesday, Nov. 26.— As soon as day-light appeared, we began to proceed forward as before, but we were all very stiff and sore. My feet swelling yet more, I got Thomas Crompton to cut my boots open in several places; they were a pair of boots which I had to Davis' Straits for seven years, and being so hard, they would scarcely bend to my feet. My right hand being frozen, and the middle finger of my left hand nearly crushed off, I was not able to unbutton my clothes without the assistance of my shipmate Taylor, whom I was obliged to ask to unbutton and button them for me. The master's hands being very much frozen, he got Crompton to assist him on with his gloves; several times his knees were much torn and lacerated, yet I never heard him complain of his feet, but I perceived his bodily health declining fast, not being able to eat much of the pork, nor were any of us except Taylor and Simpson, who could sit down and eat as hearty as if it had been meat that was cooked.

We travelled on the most part of the day, but nothing could be discovered like a house or habitation to shelter us in this inclement season. Mr. Collinson observed, that he was afraid it was a judgment the Lord had sent upon us for leaving Webster. We travelled to a high cliff that projected out; here we all stood looking with great anxiety to the westward, but nothing could we discover but high mountains; as bad or worse than any we had before passed. Nothing like the low land, or an inhabited country, could be seen. Mr. M'Cullum said, "You all plainly see there is nothing for us but returning back to the wreck, as the boat is the only hope we have now left, if it should please the Lord to enable us to reach it."

As such, we came to the conclusion to return, and we from this time and place began to return to the wreck which we had left. The master was yet inclined to have gone forward, and he added, "I am certain I shall never live to reach the wreck." The answer I made to our much beloved master was, "O yes, sir, if it please God, I hope you will; it is a very trying circumstance to think of; we know indeed what we have passed through in coming hither, and the thoughts of having the same trials to pass through again, is indeed, sir, enough almost to break one's heart." The master said, "You told me you would endeavour to get a fire." We sat down to try if possible to get one; having obtained two of the dryest sticks we could find, two of our companions, who were the best able, viz. Crompton and the pilot, set to work, and rubbed the sticks together till they were almost exhausted, but to no effect; they could make plenty of smoke, but no fire. I told them the way we used to do at Greenland, with a thowl, a snow shovel, and a fox, things which are well known to an old Greenlandman.— We tried every means we could devise, but to no purpose, every thing about us being so very wet and damp, that there was no possibility of obtaining a fire; some of our company put a piece of old shirt in their bosoms to dry it, afterwards they would tease it to tow, but all without effect. Crompton had picked up a piece of flint, by the help of which and his knife we fondly hoped we should gain a light. We worked on very hard for a long time, but all in vain, every thing being against us, in regard to getting a light, or obtaining fire. We got up again, and proceeded on our journey, but all very stiff and sore.

I only once recollect seeing one or two land birds all the time we were travelling. The master observing them, said, "Oh, you pretty little things, I think I could eat one of you;" scarcely any thing to be seen alive in the woods at this season of the year. Our companions by this time had got some distance from us, the master likewise had got a little before me, and when I got up to him, he exclaimed, "Oh dear, Mr. Burrows, I am sure we shall never be able to get back to the wreck." I said to him, in reply, if we did, I was pretty certain I should lose the use of some of my limbs; my feet felt frozen to a solid mass, and no movement in the ankle joints. Mr. Collinson said, "I wish we could find some place to lie down in, for I am sure I cannot proceed much further."

The rest of our companions being at a small distance from us, they stopped till we reached them, and they said they should endeavour if possible to reach the place where we stopped last night; and, as darkness was fast approaching, they all went on except Mr. M'Cullum, the master, and myself. Mr. Collinson said, "Mr. Burrows, I cannot get any further." Where we were at this time situated, there was a small crag in the rocks, by the side of the mountain, and to get up this the master and I were too weak. Mr. M'Cullum said, "Do my good men, if it be possible, try to get on further." I said, "Mr. M'Cullum, you plainly see the master can get no further. Oh my good man, for God's sake, don't leave us; you may as well stop with us here for the present, as you must perceive we cannot proceed any farther." Mr. Collinson said, "You know that I and the mate were worn out before the ship came on shore." We sat down together; Mr. M'Cullum went to cut down branches from the trees to make our bed, it being a very wet and snowy night. Sometimes the pilot walked up and down, and at other times lay down beside us. So extreme were our sufferings, that the night was spent by us with very little conversation. There fell so much snow upon us from the trees, that we were wet to the skin, which caused us to tremble and shake all night long. Towards day-light, we heard the rest of our companions, and we thought we were not far from them.

Thursday being the 27th, the fourth day from our having left the wreck, we got up, but were very ill able to stand, and got a drink of water. Mr. M'Cullum said, "Come, let us try to get to the rest of our companions." The master replied, "I know I cannot get much further, and I am sure I shall never live to reach the wreck." He spoke this in a very faint low tone of voice; he looked most shockingly in the face, and likewise, to all appearance, failed, and was shrunk very much in the body. How I looked I know not, but I did not find myself so very bad in the body; yet what is the use of the body, abstractedly considered, when the feet and hands are useless? Mr. M'Cullum was always very nimble and quick in walking.

We got to the rest of our comrades, and partook of a little of the pork, but the master was not able to eat any. We went to a stream and kneeled down, and all drank heartily of the water, and then began to go forward as well as could be expected in the state we were all in. Shortly after this, we reached the stream where we left the keg which held our small stock of spirits; we put water into it, and drank thereof for the sake of the spirit that was in it.

We went on with heavy hearts and trembling limbs the greatest part of this day, the master and myself making several stoppages to rest ourselves, not being able to keep up with the rest of our companions; at length the master became so very bad, he said, in a voice that was scarcely audible, "I can proceed no further." Mr. M'Cullum said, "The Lord have mercy upon you, poor man! If we cannot get on, we must all very soon perish and die: I fear we shall be obliged to leave you"; this was repeated several times. One of the men also said, "Capt. Collinson we cannot stop any longer here, we shall all be starved to death." He answered, "My good friend, you should recollect and not so soon forget what I have done for you, (alluding to the circumstance of attending him and lowering him from the top, and cherishing him on the day of the wreck) I can clap my hand upon my heart and say, I never hurt a man in my life."

Mr. Collinson got but very little further. Mr. M'Cullum said, "Mr. Collinson, God help you poor man! I see you can get no further; would you like to give us your ring, that, if it please God any of us should survive and reach home, we may give it to your father or brother?" Mr. Collinson never made any reply that I heard of, but he looked most shockingly. I had not power to speak to him, and I was aware there was no possibility of getting the ring off, as his fingers were so much frozen and swelled with the cold. I put my head into a hole in the rock to get a drink, where there was but just room to get the head in and out; my companions all did in like manner, but I do not think the master would have had power to get his head out had they not assisted him. We had not had any water for some time, and were all very thirsty.

The master at this time began to be quite delirious; he raved and talked extremely wild; the closing scene with him appeared to be fast approaching. The last time I heard him speak, he called "William Rose," and this name he repeated several times. I had not heard him speak of William Rose since about three hours before the ship struck and went on shore. I particularly mention this, because I think it was remarkable, and indicated the rapid approach of death. The time he spoke of this young man was, when we close reefed the main topsail; he said to me he was as clever and active a young man as any we had in the ship, and we were all aware that the master knew him to have been drowned from the vessel. The mentioning of this young man's name were Mr. Collinson's last words.

Thus ended the mortal existence of our much respected master, after having been exposed to innumerable hardships and suffering, in the bloom of youth, upon a barren inhospitable part of the Island of Cape Breton, and far remote from his family and friends, and every thing he held most dear. I stood by him awhile, a silent spectator of his sufferings, and expecting I should be the next to drop off. Thomas Crompton cut down some fir branches to cover him. I thought within myself, I have now no alternative left, I must either stop and die, beside the master, or I must go on with my companions in distress. Mr. M'Cullum said to me, "Will you be able to proceed?" I replied, I would try to get on as well as I possibly could. We then pressed forward, and left Mr. Collinson behind us. I thought I heard him groan or cry oh! or something to that effect. I am certain, might I have had the whole island for barely carrying the master's hat, it would have been totally out of my power, my hands and feet being so very much frozen. We went on with very heavy hearts for the loss of our master, stopping at night as before, and sleeping amongst the snow.

We arose in the morning of the 28th in a most deplorable condition indeed. We had not gone far before I found myself left behind by the rest of my companions, except Thomas Crompton, who scarcely ever left me out of hearing. I always found the feet marks of my comrades in the snow. I was attempting to run, when I thought I heard them call and shout of me, which made me double my exertions; but every stump of a tree or stone my feet struck against threw me down, almost enough to break all my ribs. One time I fell down with my face in the snow, and there I thought I could lie and die; I fell asleep for a few moments, but I soon awoke as if one had roused me up. I went on following the footsteps of my companions: I soon heard Crompton shouting of me, which gave me great encouragement to go on.

I got to a large fall of water coming down from the mountains; the sight of this place gave me great trouble of mind, not knowing how I should get over, being unable to skip from one rock to another. I knew if I slipt, there was such a heavy fall of water, I should never get out again. I went down the side of it, till at length I saw a large tree that had broken down and had fallen over the river, and Crompton on the opposite side waiting for me. I got upon the tree with my breast, and with my arms worked myself across to the other side. Soon after I got up to Crompton, and kept his company for a short time. To this friend I was particularly indebted; had it not been for his kind attention and assistance, I should never have reached the wreck. Towards night, I came up with the rest of my companions. It was a happy circumstance that we always found plenty of water wherever we stopped, either for the night or to rest ourselves. This was the chief of our support. The pork was become very dirty with dragging through the bushes and snow; and, having all the hair upon it, it was almost past eating the latter part of our journey.

On the 29th, in the afternoon, we got to the wreck, and there we found poor Webster in the same place where we left him. He appeared to be in better health than we were who had been travelling. His heart leaped for joy at the sight of us; he had lost a great deal of blood; the grass where he had laid was covered therewith. He told us the other pig came close round him several times since we left him. We related to him the awful tale of the sufferings and ultimate loss of Mr. Collinson, which he was very sorry to hear.

Sunday the 30th, blowing strong, with snow and much sea on, there was no possibility of doing any thing with the boat. When I got laid, or sat down, in the bower of nature's forming in the rock, I was not able to rise up.— Some of our companions went down to the wreck, and on their way found a few cranberries, but no provisions.— This day was spent by us all in a most bemoaning state, expecting we should not be able to get the boat over the timber into the water, as there was a great deal of lumber in the way.

Monday, Dec. 1st, light airs from the eastward, but, for this season of the year, fine weather. We went down to the boats, or I may rather say respecting some, they crawled down, to use our utmost endeavours to get her out. With large rickers, at length we got her from the inside of the long boat, and by laying spars across the timber, and shoving her broadside first by little and little, some of us on our knees the whole time, at length, with the assistance of the Lord, we succeeded in getting her into the water, for which we had all great reason to be thankful. It was a matter of great gratitude to the Almighty, that two of our companions had retained so much of their strength, or we should never have got her out.

The boat we found leaked much. We discovered a drawer belonging to a chest, which served to bail her with, and a pail which we filled with fresh water; we also found a hammock which we made a mainsail of, and a large rug which made us a foresail; and we put in some old copper, which came off the ship's bottom, for ballast. Crompton saw one oar in a cove to the eastward, which he went for, but was scarcely able to bring it to the boat, and we were so fortunate as to find part of another; with these we thought we might be able to pull along the boat with the assistance of the sails. The next consideration was, how we should be able to get the cook into the boat, which we could not determine; however, with much exertion, he crept on his knees into it. We saw the other pig several times come very nigh us, but none of us were able to go after him.

With a fresh breeze, and thus equipped, we left the awful place. We run along side the land to the westward, Taylor constantly bailing the boat; with respect to myself, I laid in the midships; Mr. M'Cullum was employed in steering; Crompton sat near him; Simpson and Webster laid in the bow, and I do not remember them ever moving much till we arrived at the settlement. Towards midnight we had calm but thick weather. I went aft and took a spell at steering; Mr. M'Cullum and Crompton took the oars. We pulled close in under the land, but did not remain long there before we thought it advisable to pull out in the offing, fearful of the wind coming on the land; and it was well for us that we did so, for shortly after the wind came nearly on the land, with very thick showers of snow.

Towards day-light in the morning of the 2d of December, the wind changed more to the eastward, with a strong breeze and much sea. Taylor still employed bailing,

Crompton and M'Cullum pulling at intervals. On this day, towards meridian, with fresh gales and a high sea, we saw the low land of Cheticamp. I told the company I saw a house, but they would not believe it. We were very fearful of running down into the bite, as the sea was so high; so we kept right for the point. [M'Cullum told Taylor if he saw a house he would give him a guinea, but that he never got; we received half a gallon of rum in lieu of it.]

In opening the point, we discovered a vessel's masts, which we thought appeared like a galliot, but we soon found her to be a ship on shore. We run for her, when she proved to be the *Commerce*, of Bristol; she had run in there full of water, and was a complete wreck. When we reached her, the mate and some of the crew came into our boat, and pulled her on shore. They took us to the house, carrying us all on their backs, except Crompton, who was the only one that hopped in. It was a fishing-house and store-house belonging to one Captain Breeho, who, we were informed, was at Guernsey, but he had a clerk who kept the store-house in his absence.[1] We were all kindly received by the storekeeper; he gave us the best refreshment he had in the house, but, having to go out to work in the day-time, he could render us no assistance except at nights. I had the boots cut off my feet, and we had our feet put into buckets of cold water for a considerable time, but to no effect. We were all put into a room, and laid on the floor on an old sail. There came to us a kind-hearted Irish woman and several others; she made us some oatmeal gruel, and put oatmeal poultices on my hands, and dressed all our feet with scraped potatoes.[2] The mate of the *Commerce* also was kind to us in rendering us every assistance in his power.

Dec. 3d, in the morning, our kind friend, the Irish woman, came again to see us, and brought her husband

1. Notes and Sources begin on page 103.

along with her. They and their family were the only persons resident here, except French people. They brought with them some milk; she made us gruel for breakfast, and likewise dressed our feet, and my hands also. The pilot having reserved some money, it began to speak the old language, and he agreed with the woman to take him to her house for the winter; he told the master of the house to give us half a gallon of rum, and then he took his leave of us, and I have never seen him since.

Webster lay in a most deplorable condition; the bones of his legs were eaten through, and limbs all swelled as thick as his thigh, and were very black and frozen. He complained sorely of lying on the hard boards; they got him some straw to lie on.

There also came to the same house the crew of the *Assistance*, of Liverpool, that left Mirimichi on Sunday morning, 23d November. The mate and part of the crew proceeded in the long boat towards the Gut of Canso, and the master and the other part of the crew remained here. This ship was wrecked on the 24th of November, the day after they sailed, as they told us; they had been joined by the crew of a schooner bound to Mirimichi from Quebec, which was wrecked near the *Assistance*, and had two officers of the army as passengers on board. They travelled to the Gut to get to Pictou, but they never came in to see us.

In this deplorable condition we lay on the hard floor for several days, the man belonging to the house having his work to attend to, and having no woman servant in the house, we could have no assistance till he came home at night. This made me lament much the loss of our master, as he would have been able to have drawn money, and relieved us by getting us a bed to lie on. We were at length relieved by one Mr. Blanchard, a Roman Catholic minister of the settlement of Cheticamp, which was about three miles distant.[3] He went round amongst his parishioners, who were all French people, and got them to take us. In a day or two, they and their worthy priest came with horses to remove us; they brought with them rugs and blankets to cover us with. They could speak but very little English; however the first that spoke to me was one Joseph Macknall, (*probably MacNeil*) who said "Will you come to my house?" I readily answered, "Yes," being desirous of getting a bed to lie on.

I was put upon his horse, and covered with blankets; so were all my shipmates, except Crompton. The man of the house told him he would keep him, as he thought he would be likely soon to recover. I then left my shipmates, and went with my guide, Joseph Macknall; he led the horse with one hand and held me on with the other. It blew and snowed very heavy, which cut my poor legs up very much, not being able to hold with my hands; and having been for some time in a warm house, and now coming out into the cold, it cut me up more than all the rest. I thought I should have fallen off the horse several times before we reached his house; at length we arrived, and I was kindly received by the mistress and daughters. I was put into a crib, made of rough slabs, upon a straw bed, which I found very comfortable, having been so long destitute, and the crib was placed alongside of a window. I found none in the house that could speak English, except the master of the house.

I was in a most deplorable condition the time I was here, having juniper poultices applied to my hands and feet every night and morning; several Indian women came in to dress my hands and feet. I was in a violent fever for several days, and was almost induced to think every day that came would be my last. Having so much fever, I was parched with thirst, and was always wanting to drink water, which was the only beverage the house afforded; and if I put it in the window during the night, it would be all ice when I wanted to drink again. The rain and snow came rattling and beating upon me in the night. I mentioned this to the master of the house, so every night afterwards they dragged the bed before the fire.

My middle finger on my left hand was now very bad, nothing left but the bone; I wished the Indian women to cut it off, but none in the house would perform this operation. I got my host to sharpen my penknife, and I cut it off myself; if I had not, it is most probable I should have lost my whole hand, as my arm was very much swelled and inflamed at the time.

One of the Indian women went into the wood and got some red kind of bark, and chewed it in her mouth to make a poultice of it for my hands. I said to the master and mistress of the house, when they were dressing my feet, "Do you think I shall lose my feet?" They always answered "O no"; but I was soon led to conclude differently. As they were taking the poultices off one night, they tore all the skin and toe nails off together; then, by painful experience, I soon found I should lose my feet, the right foot being slewed athwart.

The master of the house went to one Ubier Auquin,[4] where Webster, the cook, resided, and he informed me on his return that they were going to cut Webster's legs off in a short time. He sent me word by the master that I was to keep up my spirits. In a few days after this he visited him again, and found that Webster had received the sacrament at the hands of the priest. Finding there was no means of saving him but by cutting his leg off, and having neither doctor nor surgeon, they engaged the most skilful person they had in the place, who, with a common joiner's saw and a large knife, took his leg off, but it not bleeding, he died shortly after. They had him decently buried by the priest in their own church yard.[5]

Shortly after this, the priest came to visit me, and brought me a Prayer Book, half English and half French, and expressed a wish for me to turn Catholic, which I told him I could not conscientiously do, wishing to abide by the religion in which I was brought up. I told him the Lord had preserved me stedfast thus far, and I hoped he would keep me stedfast to the end of my days. He asserted our religion was good for nothing; that every thing that Martin Luther or Mr. Wesley were the instruments of propagating were dangerous tenets. I told him that what they advanced they gathered from the revealed will of God in the Scriptures of truth. He also said, the Bible itself was not good without proper explanations. He told me we had too many religions in England; that the Lord only instituted one religion, and that is ours, or the Catholic faith. He said to me, "You are very ill indeed, I am of an opinion that you will not get better." I answered, "Well, sir, the Lord is sufficient for all things, and he can restore me if it be his good will and pleasure so to do."

In a day or two after, the mate of the *Commerce* came in to see me, and gave me half a dollar, which I gave to the master of the house to take care of for me, and which he did, for my tobacco pouch and this money I never saw after. While I was at this house, two men came to enquire if I was willing that the boat should be sold; they said they would give five pouuds for her, and a Peter O'Quin was to pay us, or let us have any thing we were in want of out of his stores instead of money.[6] This proposal was agreed to, as I thought these things would be serviceable some time, should we get better; but in this I was much deceived, as I never received a farthing's worth of any thing for my share of it. Here also I saw Esquire Mickanin,[7] a justice of the peace from Margree, which was about thirty miles distant.

At this house I remained about a fortnight; the person who lived in it had a large family and was very poor, and of course was not able to keep me long. My living here was chiefly a little barley soup and tea, but I scarcely ever tasted bread. The master of the house was very kind; he served me every meal, as I was unable to assist myself. On Sunday the 21st December, to the best of my recollection, as he gave me my breakfast, he told me I was about to be removed to another person's house who had more meat than he had, and of course could provide better for me, and he said the priest thought I should live better there. In a little time, Wm. Budrow[8] came with the priest's horse and carryall; I was put therein, my right foot nearly mortified off and my left one in a bad putrified state, and then covered with blankets. We soon got to my new lodgings. I was immediately put into a bed, laid on the floor close to the fire; this bed had more room in it, and was much softer and more comfortable than the crib which I had at the other house. My new master gave me some refreshment, the best which he had. The women here were always willing to do all they could for me. When his son began to dress my feet, they were in a sad putrid state, so much so, that he soon grew tired of dressing them and my hands. At his house the steward of the *Assistance* lodged for the winter. This man gave me every assistance in his power; he came regularly to dress my feet and hands every night, which gave me great comfort. One night I said "John, (that was his christian name) I think my right foot is nearly off." In the morning, Charles Budrow cut it off and buried it in the garden.

After this time, two books kept me engaged at intervals in reading for several months, when I got able to sit up in bed; they were the *Common Prayer* and Bunyan's *Pilgrim's Progress*, and were a great comfort to me, as they seemed to ease my pains and sufferings, and made the time pass on sweeter than it would have done otherwise. A short time after this, there came to this house one Mr. Duffice,[9] and another gentleman, from Brasdor,[10] and

Mr. Mickanin, from Margree; they came to the sale of the
ship *Commerce*, and lodged at this house two or three
days. I said to Mr. Duffice, "Would you be so kind, sir, as
to inform me how I might procure a protest to send to the
owner?"— He said, "You must apply to Mr. Mickanin,
and I will also speak to him for you."

The next morning Mr. Mickanin came to me to take
down the particulars. He said he could not make the
protest out there, as he had business to transact at the
point, and he would wish to see the pilot and the other
men belonging to the ship.— When he had got the protest
made out, he said he would come to me, which he did in a
day or two after. He read the protest to me; I told him I
did not think it was altogether correct; he told me it would
do very well, and, having the pen stuck in the handerchief
that bound up my hand, I was enabled to sign it, at least
to make a mark, as I could not possibly write. I said, "Mr.
Mickanin, you said you would write me a letter to my
wife." He said, "So I will, but I cannot stop to do it now."

When I saw him about a fortnight afterwards, he told
me he had forwarded the protest, and also the letter, to
Mr. Duffice, and he had no doubt but he would forward
them to Halifax in due course. He said, if I lived to get to
England, he hoped I would put his name in the paper, as he
wished to get to be an agent for Lloyds. He must have for-
got or neglected his engagement, as neither the protest nor
the letter ever reached England. He asked me if I was
agreeable for the wreck of the ship, which still remained on
the shore, to be sold. I told him, if it would fetch any small
matter that would do us good, I had no objection. He accordingly gave notice at four o'clock, and at six it was sold.
Three Frenchmen came to the sale, but there being only
two bidders, Mr. Mickanin bought it in himself for two
guineas, and told me Peter O'Quin was either to pay the
money, or let us have any thing we wanted to the amount.

At this house several Frenchmen used to come to spend an hour or two on Sunday between the times of service, and by this means I frequently got to know how my shipmates came on. They told me Taylor had had his foot cut off. I enquired whether it was removed with a knife. They replied, "Yes, with a pen-knife." One of these persons informed me John Simpson was in a very bad state; he had lost one of his feet, and he was very fearful he should soon lose the other. The old man and his wife always left me alone the most part of the Sunday, and the steward of the *Assistance*, who lived at the son's house, at the next door, always came in to bear me company. One night, as the steward was dressing my legs, he said, "This foot is very nigh off"; I said, "Yes, it is; if you will give me the razor I will cut it off." I cut two or three of the leaders, and down it dropt, but it never bled a single drop; had I let it be a day or two longer, it must have dropped off of itself.— Charles Budrow took it and buried it in the garden with the other.

One night I was informed that some Frenchmen had been down as far as our wreck; they were travelling in the woods, and found my leather jacket. I asked them if they saw any thing of the remains of our master; they said they saw nothing in their whole journey but a dead bear, stuck fast between two trees. Mr. Mickanin obliged them to give me my leather jacket. One evening the steward told me I was going to be removed to another house.— I asked him where to; he said, to Mr. Chessong's; I heard them speak of it last night; he understood French a little.

On the 2d of March, 1824, Joseph Chessong[11] came for me with the priest's horse and carryall; I was put in and covered up. He said to me as we were going, "I shall keep you till the month of May, and take you to Pictou in my shallop." I said, "How far is your house off"; he told me five miles; the name of the place was Little River (*the old name for the Cheticamp River*). Our road lay through the wood, and with driving over tree roots; it was sometimes fit to heave me out. We at length got there, and I was kindly received by all in the house; my legs were much swelled. The family consisted of two sons; one was married, and had two children, but not one of the family could speak a word of English except the master of the house, and he but very little. In these good people I found both a father and a mother; no son could be treated with more kindness than I was by this family. The priest often came to dine with them; one day he said to me, "How do you like these people"; I answered, "Very well indeed." I afterwards found it was through his goodness I was removed hither.

While I was at the other house, I was told by Mr. Mickanin that he would remit me some money to enable me to reach Pictou, but I scarcely ever saw Mr. Mickanin afterwards. In this situation Edward Taylor lodged very near me, a man of the name of Christopher Temple, and another called Mitchell. The two last belonged to the crew of the *Assistance*. The people were always telling me, if my ankle bones were cut off, my legs would very soon be well; so I spoke to the master of the house one night, as I was getting my legs dressed, requesting him to cut them off for me. The old woman shook her head at this, and her husband told me the priest had given a very strict charge to them not to cut any thing whatever belonging to me, and I found they would not go against his orders on any account. I said, "If you will get me the saw, I will cut them off myself, or get Mitchell to remove the bones for me." He replied, "You may do as you think proper, but we will have no hand in cutting you: I will procure you the saw to-morrow if possible."

Accordingly, in three or four days the saw was obtained, and I sent for Mitchell and Temple, who came. Mitchell sawed one of my ankle bones off from the left leg, but he haggled it very much, (the women all ran out): it bled profusely, but that was soon stopped by the application of fuzball. The next night I got the saw; there was a piece of the ankle bone on the right leg, but the flesh prevented my cutting it all off.

Here Temple always came to stop with Taylor or me every day, so one of us always had his company. The time I was here, my legs being much inflamed, they applied dog-fish oil to them, and salve that the priest had received from Sidney. I found Mr. Duffice had been as good as his word, as he had raised a subscription in Sidney, and the French people were to have half a dollar a day for keeping us all. I told Temple to request Peter O'Quin to send me a bottle of rum to wash my legs with, and send the rest of the balance due to me in clothes or any thing else. He brought me the rum, and told me that Peter O'Quin said there was nothing more due to me; where I last lived the people had got the principal part of what was due, after Mr. Mickanin was paid a guinea, which he charged for the protest. I was informed that Smith, the pedlar, was gone with twenty men to try to get what he could from the wreck of our ship, in which he proved successful, and found several of the dead bodies of our crew, and buried them, putting a handspike with the ship's name branded upon it, which served as a head-stone.

On Tuesday the 18th of May, Mr. Chessong informed me they were going to Pictou, and Mr. Blanchard was going part of the way with us. I was put on a truck and covered with blankets, which the kind-hearted old lady made me a present of. When I got down to the beach I saw my old shipmates Simpson and Taylor, whom I had not seen for nearly six months; we were all put on board of different shallops, so that I had not the opportunity of speaking to them till we arrived at Pictou. My good old lady made the bed and got me into it, before she left me that night.

After we sailed from Cheticamp, I found kind treatment from the hand of the good priest; he frequently gave me a little wine. On the 19th, at night, we put him on shore at a small village on the island of St. John's; on the 20th of May we arrived at Pictou. The master of the shallops went to see if the merchants would allow us to be taken on shore; on his return he informed us that the merchants said they should have taken us to Halifax. All the shallop masters came on board, and said they were afraid we were going to be worse treated than we had been by them. I enquired of Mr. Chessong who was the justice of the peace there; he told me Mr. Smith. In the morning I wrote to him, and Mr. Chessong took the letter; he immediately sent him on board to get the vessels under weigh, and come alongside the quay. He had us all conveyed to a house, and Doctor Johnson was sent to dress our limbs; he being the first real doctor we had fallen in with. I was the first that he began to dress; he took out the remaining part of my ankle bone; it was very mouldy in the inside, having been so severely frozen.— I told him about cutting them; he said if I had left them alone, they would all have come out in the same way, and if he had been with us in the winter, he would not have left one leg amongst us all, but would have made a complete cure of us. He also dressed the other men's legs, and he gave orders to the people of the house to let us want for nothing. In a day or two Mr. Smith, the magistrate, came to see me, and on his return sent me a suit of his own clothes, and I hope he will never know want for his great kindness.

We sometimes heard we were likely to be sent to Halifax, but in a short time they came to a conclusion that we should remain there, and a subscription was set on foot for our relief in all the churches and chapels, and also among the shipping, which consisted of about thirty sail; not a master, man, or scarcely a boy, but who gave three or four shillings each, and I heard in all there was nearly sixty pounds collected. But what with our board and the doctor's bill, and the relief of several other shipwrecked mariners, who were all paid out of this subscription, there was but a small quantity of dollars came into our hands.

Crompton had so far recovered as to be able to look out for a ship for himself, and went with the first ship which sailed for England. The master of the house, a tavern keeper, of the name of Cummins, charged a guinea per week for each of our board, and the principal part of the week our provisions were salt herring and potatoes; we did not like to make this known to our doctor, or I am of opinion he would have remedied it. We were told by a person, that Capt. Lowrie, of the *Barbara*, would probably take one of us to England; we told Simpson he had better endeavour to see him, and speak to him upon the subject. He went upon his knees to his office, and found him, and having engaged with the gentleman who held the subscription money, he took him for five pounds. Simpson gave me the preference of going in his stead, but I told him that as Capt. Gill, of the *Dixon*, had promised to take me, I would stop for him, as he was bound direct to Hull, so that Simpson left in that ship for Newcastle direct. We heard there was some money sent to Pictou for our relief from Halifax, obtained by the exhibition of an Indian chief's head, which put us in possession of a few shillings more than our shipmate Simpson got. The *Dixon* and the *Neptune* being the only Hull ships, we naturally expected we might have been sent home in them, but they went to take in the remainder of their cargoes at Tattamagush, and after a short time, I was informed they were loaded; I therefore left Taylor, and told him I was determined, if possible, to go to Mr. Smith's, to know if we could not be sent to Tattamagush to be in readiness to go on board those vessels.

On my knees I managed to reach Mr. Smith's residence, and his clerk informed me that Mr. Smith was ill in bed, but upon the business being made known to him, he sent word down that those two ships had sailed, and they never had been able with convenience to get us down there; that we should now be obliged to stop and go with Capt. Hobbart, in the *Enterprize*, as he had promised to take us all three, if we did not meet with a conveyance before he sailed. Of course Taylor and I now had nothing else to depend upon. Accordingly, when the ship was ready, we were taken on board, and I was informed he was to have seven pounds for each of us for our passage.

On the 14th of July, to the best of my recollection, we sailed from Pictou on board the *Enterprize*, bound for Liverpool. Mr. Hobbart behaved to us with the greatest civility, but being under the necessity of sleeping on a straw bed, having nothing to cover us with upon the wet timber, and nearly under the forecastle hatchway, we had but very uncomfortable lodgings. On our passage Taylor expressed a wish to me to get into the hospital at Liverpool; I told him I would stop in Liverpool till he had gained admission, and then I would reach Hull if possible. Capt. Hobbart told us on our passage that he would use his utmost endeavours to raise a subscription for us in Liverpool.

On our arrival, which was on the 14th day of August, Capt. Hobbart was as good as his word; a friend of his, Mr. Hodgson, a timber merchant, had us conveyed to a Mrs. Knowle's, in Crosley-street, and in three or four days he got Taylor admitted into the hospital. I gave Mr. Hodgson a brief account of our shipwreck and subsequent misfortunes, who very warmly espoused our cause, and was indefatigable in his exertions to obtain us all the relief in his power, wherever he could get us a shilling he willingly went; indeed the kindness of this gentleman cannot be adequately expressed. By his desire I stopped in Liverpool till the 30th of August, when I took my leave of him and Mr. Hobbart, who was the means of our introduction to him, and on Thursday the 2d of September, I arrived in Hull, having been nearly twelve months absent, above nine months of which I experienced, with the rest of my fellow-sufferers, a complicated series of afflictions which cannot be described.

After all I feel I have much cause to be thankful to the Almighty for his preserving goodness, and for raising me up such kind friends, not only in Liverpool but in Hull, many who have not only felt for our sufferings and sympathized in our distress, but have generously come forward to help us; and I hope and trust I shall never forget the kindness of all those friends who have contributed even in the smallest degree to my relief and that of my fellow-sufferers. I trust their kindness will never be erased from my grateful recollection.[12]

THE END of Samuel Burrows' *Narrative*

NOTES & SOURCES
to Samuel Burrows' *Narrative*

Most of the following notes are based on research by Cheticamp genealogist Charles D. Roach (C. D. R.).

1. "Captain Breeho is no doubt Captain Briard who, at the time, lived at the Point, on Cheticamp Island, and is known to have operated a store there. He was originally from the Channel Islands (Jersey and Guernsey)." C. D. R.

2. It is interesting to note the number of home remedies used throughout Samuel Burrows' account. The "kind-hearted Irish woman" put oatmeal poultices on his hands and dressed everyone's frozen feet with scraped potatoes. Juniper poultices are used, and an Indian woman collected red bark, chewed it for a poultice. A fuzball is used to stop bleeding. Dog-fish oil is applied to Burrows' inflamed legs as well as a salve the priest got from Sydney. Later, Burrows rubbed his legs with rum.

3. "Mr. Blanchard is Burrows' memory of the name of Rev. Augustin Magloire Blanchet, the first parish priest of Cheticamp." C. D. R.

4. "Ubier Aucoin is certainly Hubert Aucoin. There was only one Aucoin with that Christian name living in Cheticamp at the time. He was the son of Anselme (son of Pierre) Aucoin and Rose (daughter of Paul) Chiasson." C. D. R

5. "A thorough search has failed to discover a grave marker indicating the site where Mr. Webster was buried. Furthermore, there is no record in the Cheticamp parish register of his death or of his burial service. It is questionable whether Mr. Webster was given a Catholic funeral service. It is possible that he was not an adherent to the Roman Catholic faith and that the priest only gave him the last sacraments conditionally." C. D. R.

6. "Peter O'Quin may be a mistake. More than likely, the store operator would have been Peter Briard, the owner of the storehouse where the survivors of the shipwreck had first been received." C. D. R. There was a Peter Aucoin whose name appears on a list of the 14 founders of Cheticamp as O'Quin. There is no evidence, however, that he ever owned a store.

7. "The well-known justice of the peace from Margaree, Ronald

McKinnon, who drew up several legal documents in our area in the early 1800's." C. D. R.

8. "Wm. Budrow is obviously one of our Boudreau, but which one? To the best of our knowledge there was no William Boudreau living in Chetricamp in 1823. The gentleman referred to was no doubt Joseph Boudreau, son of Germain Bourdreau and Anne Hébert, married to Anne (daughter of Paul) Chiasson. This Joseph had a son named Charles. This fits with Mr. Burrows' narrative which states that Wm. Budrow had a son Charles living next door. These two Boudreau families lived in the back district of Cheticamp at a place called Le Platin, quite close to the road running through, only a few hundred feet to the southwest of the monument which now stands in memory of our 'Quatorze Vieux,' the 14 petitioners for the first land grant to the Acadians of Cheticamp." C. D. R.

9. Mr. Duffice is most likely James Duffus, the first English settler of Baddeck. He came to Cape Breton in 1819 and established a mercantile business on Mutton Island in Baddeck, renaming the island Duke of Kent's Island. He died in 1833, leaving a young widow.

According to Patterson's *History of Victoria County*, James' "executors in Halifax sent down, in 1836, a gay young captain of the militia, by name William Kidston, to look after his affairs and wind up his business." Kidston instead married Mrs. Duffus, took over the business and renamed the island Kidston's Island.

10. The other "gentleman, from Brasdor," is probably William Duffus, James' brother, who in 1824 established a branch of the Baddeck business at Big Bras d'Or.

11. "In 1823-24, there were two heads of family Chiasson by the name of Joseph in Cheticamp and both lived at Petit Etang—then often called Little River. One Joseph Chiasson was the son of Paul Chiasson and Louise Boudreau; the other was the son of Jean Chiasson (brother of Paul) and Elisabeth Boudreau (sister of Louise). Only the latter had two sons, one already married in 1824. Thus, we can conclude that Joseph Chessong is Joseph (son of Jean) Chiasson, known by the nickname Manawar (man-o'-war?), married to Marie Maillet, daughter of Grégoire (son of Jacques) Maillet and Anne (daughter of Pierre) LeBlanc." C. D. R.

12. The following Notes are grounded upon the narration of Thomas Crompton, one of the seamen of the *Wyton*, who first arrived in England, and are added to this little publication by a person deeply interested in and affected by the catastrophe they attempt to describe:

"On the dreadful Saturday night previous to the wreck of the ship, and after the fore-yard had broken, all the seamen were ordered aloft, to attempt the stowing of the fore-topsail; this was found, however, to be impossible, such was the fury of the tempest; the smaller storm sails had blown away, and in endeavouring to contend with the gale, by a press of sail, the lee side of the ship was immersed in the waves to the height of several feet up the shrouds, or as it is technically called, 'leading blocks under.' In this attempt to stow the topsail, Simpson, a seaman, one of the survivors, owing to the severity of the weather, was deprived of the use of all his limbs, and was lying in the fore-top; the master, prompted by humanity, went up aloft, and assisted in lowering him down, himself directing and guiding the rope by which he was suspended. This man was taken into the cabin, and carefully attended to; he was in bed when the ship struck upon the fatal rocks, and yet, such is the will of Providence, he escaped ashore, survived the horrors of their wanderings on this desolate shore, and lived to reach his native home.

"In the course of Sunday, it was necessary that the main-topsail should be set; being furled, with a double reef, it would require to be close reefed before this could be effected: however, owing to the exhausted state of the crew, it was deemed by them an impossibility.

"The awful moment arrived, at which our captain communicated to us that there was no hope but what the mercy of God might afford; this was four o'clock in the afternoon, and we were summoned to implore, by earnest prayer, the Almighty's aid. After prayers, it was determined by the master, that to set the main-topsail should at all events be attempted; and to convince the crew how willingly he exposed himself, and that from them he required nothing more than what he would himself endure, he went aloft along with the sailors, and took the weather yard arm, the most hazardous and exposed situation during this operation, and succeeded in reefing and setting the sail; eventually, it was of no service.

"At about half-past eight, the master told us he apprehended that the ship would strike; about this time, the second mate (who was afterwards washed away on the ship's striking) exclaimed, 'Lord have mercy upon us! there is the land!' It was a dreadful November night, and dark; the sleet and snow were driven by the wind with cutting force. The ship struck, and the waves and surf roared over her with tremendous agitation; she went forward, however, a little, and again struck, and was close to the high rocks of the shore; the sea now made a clear breach over her; the waves in lifting up our ill-fated vessel, forced her against the Beetting Rocks, and in ascending and descending, the chain plates on her sides, and the iron on her yard arms, struck fire against the rocks.

"The crew took to the rigging, the greater part of whom were washed away from thence; the captain and mate, and three or four more, were in the mizen-top, expecting every moment the ship to go over; they then came down, and the ship went over, and on the broad side of the vessel they attempted to reach the fore part, in which attempt three of them were drowned.

"The mainmast fell close to the deck; the timber with which the ship was laden was now breaking out from the bottom of the ship, and knocking about on all sides. These masses of timber, dashing about with the surf, and driven by the waves on each side of the vessel, formed between the ship and the land a sort of moveable bridge, by means of which the carpenter was the first to attempt reaching the shore; he was unfortunately dashed to pieces. The master made the next attempt, and we were ignorant of his fate; he had, however, succeeded, for I found him on the rocks, very much exhausted. The ship then fell into deep water. The moon had just risen, but the weather still continued thick with snow. I took off my clothes, and wrung the wet out of them; I also took off the master's coat, and wrung it too for him.

"We were wrecked upon the point of a headland, close to a large cove, and on the beach of this cove eight of us were now assembled; the rest of the crew and passengers, twelves in number, had met a watery grave. Their fate was melancholy; but they were spared ills and hardships worse than death itself, which were endured afterwards by us who had escaped drowning. Webster, the man who had his leg broken by the chain cable, when the ship struck, was one of the eight.

"The sea now came with such fury as to drive us away from the small portion of beach which had been the means of our rescue, and we were constrained to climb the rocks for shelter. The master and the narrator assisted the broken-legged man up a part of the height, when the master called the other men to assist, condemning them for not more readily rendering assistance to a fellow-creature in such a condition. On the top of the heights were the woods, and against the trees we stood, or paced among the snow near them, anxiously awaiting for day-light. The boy Warcup, having neither shoes nor stockings on when cast ashore, suffered dreadfully, and was delirious a part of the night. At day-light we went down to the wreck, and found a keg with a little gin in it; the master poured a little into the boy's mouth, but it was too late—death had seized the lad.

"Principally induced by the passenger, who was a resident, and, I believe, a native of the country, and the erroneous impression that the distance to a settlement did not exceed fifteen miles, it was unfortunately resolved to make the attempt to reach it by land.—Providentially, the two pigs on board the vessel were washed ashore alive, one of which was caught and killed by the master. The pig was divided into four quarters, one of which was left with the broken-legged man, and he was placed near a small stream of water, with the flesh beside him. The master assured him, that whatever hour in the night it might be when they reached the settlement, he would return for him, with the necessary means of assistance. The reader is already aware of this poor man's fate."

END of NOTES to Samuel Burrows' *Narrative*

NOTES & SOURCES
to Ensign Prenties' *Narrative*
prepared by G. G. Campbell
BM—British Museum; PAC—Public Archives of Canada

NOTES TO THE PROLOGUE

1. M. Benjamin Sulte has shown that the Golden Dog of Quebec is a copy of a similar device once to be seen in Pézenas, a village in southern France. Carved above a gateway in a stone wall, the original was dated 1561 and bore verses differing slightly from those in the Quebec inscription:

> Je suis un chien qui ronge l'os
> En le rongeant je prends repos.
> Un temps viendra qui n'est venu
> Ou je mordrai qui m'a mordu.

According to local tradition, a one-time owner of the property enclosed by the stone wall had a plantation of orange trees that was coveted by a local grandee. When the owner refused to part with his orchard, his powerful neighbour had the trees removed by night and re-planted on his own property. In a day when an ordinary man could not with impunity challenge the great and powerful, the owner of the trees contented himself with erecting the menacing device for all to see.

More than one man, as M. Sulte makes clear, impressed the verses on his memory. One who did so was Timouthée Roussel, surgeon, born not far from Pézenas. Roussel made his way to Canada and settled in Quebec. In 1688 he erected the stone house on rue Buade. Recalling as best he could the device he had seen in Pézenas, he had a copy made for his new house. His memory, however, was faulty; whereas the orig-inal verses were metrically correct, Roussel's version is not, though it does convey the meaning of the original. (See B. Sulte: *Le Chien D'or*, in *Bulletins Recherches historiques*, Vol. XXI, pp. 270 ff.)

2. William Kirby's novel, *The Golden Dog*, was published in 1877.

3. Alice, only daughter of Miles and Elizabeth Prenties, married George Sproule in 1769. The marriage is on record in the Archives Judiciaires, Quebec.

Ensign Sproule, 59th Regiment, was on garrison duty in Louisbourg when, in 1765, Captain Samuel Holland arrived in Cape Breton to be-gin his survey of the island. Sproule volunteered for service with the survey party, and showed such aptitude that Holland had him ap-pointed to his permanent staff. Sproule's plan of ruined Louisbourg, made in 1767, is in the Archives of the Fortress of Louisbourg. Much of the Bras d'Or complex was mapped by a party under his direction. When Holland completed his work in Cape Breton, he took Sproule with him to Quebec, where the young man met and married Alice Prenties. In 1770 Holland and his staff moved to New Hampshire, and there George Sproule made his home. The Revolution drove him from his holdings, and it was as a Loyalist refugee that he arrived in Fredericton, New Brunswick. He was made Surveyor General of that province in 1784, and died after 1810. (See D. C. Harvey: *Holland's Description of Cape Breton Island...* A publication of the Public Ar-chives of Nova Scotia.)

4. According to Prenties, he purchased his commission in July, 1778, with money provided by his father. (Prenties to Haldimand in PAC, Haldimand Papers, B. 72, p. 232.)

5. PAC, Haldimand Papers, B. 213, pp. 83-84: *Memorial of Ensn Prenties of the 84th Regiment*. The early stages of Prenties' troubled army career can be traced in letters passing between headquarters and regimental officers, headquarters and Haldimand, Haldimand and

Prenties. See Haldimand Papers, B. 61, p. 44; B. 80, pp. 205 & 210; B. 129, pp. 89-91; B. 147, p. 276; B. 82, pp. 4-6; B. 73, pp. 232 & 145.

NOTES TO THE NARRATIVE

6. The only shoals and reefs to be found near Prenties' estimated distance from shore are those jutting from Margaree Island. The *St. Lawrence* must have driven shoreward past the thunderous surf that assails the island in big storms. The island is one and a quarter miles in length, and lies parallel to the shore at a distance of two and a half miles.

7. Under the title, "Prenties Delivers his Despatches," Archibald MacMechan included an account of Prentiess experience in his *Sagas of the Sea* (J. M. Dent & Sons, 1923). Dr. MacMechan, on grounds that are not clear, believed the *St. Lawrence* went ashore near Little Judique Ponds. The evidence does not support his belief.

In the first place, while the captain of the *St. Lawrence* may have been a sot, he was also trained and experienced in navigation. He had no trouble in identifying St. John's Island, with whose coastal peculiarities he showed himself to be familiar. If his ship had landed in the Judique area, the trend of the coast and the sight of mainland Nova Scotia across St. George's Bay would have told him instantly that he was near the entrance to the Strait of Canso. He would have known, too, that the shortest way to Louisbourg, where help could be found, was south through the strait. That the captain turned north from the place of shipwreck is clear evidence that he believed himself to be even nearer the tip of Cape Breton than he actually was.

The *Narrative*, moreover, supplies proof that Margaree Harbour was the scene of the shipwreck. The first three localities at which the ship's boat put ashore after leaving the wreck can be identified with certainty from Prenties' descriptions. The distance between the first of these and Margaree Harbour corresponds very closely with Prenties' estimate of the first day's journey northward from the wreck; Prenties would be out by more than forty miles if the wreck lay at Judique.

8. The Margaree is not an ordinary river. Its longer branch takes its rise eight miles east of Chéticamp, in Cape Breton's most elevated region, flows for twenty miles parallel to the coast in a southwesterly direction, then turns about to join the other branch and run north-north-west to meet the sea at Margaree Harbour. This peculiar behaviour results from the fact that the present river-system was once two

completely separate systems. In one of these, the main river, a conse-
quent stream, followed the south-easterly slope of the ancient Atlantic
Upland through the wind-gap now occupied by the Lakes of Law. In
the other system, the main stream took its rise near the present Lake
Ainslie and flowed a course almost parallel to that of the first stream,
but in the opposite direction. For thousands of years, stream piracy
worked inexorably to divert into the second system two major tributaries of the first stream—Gallant River and Big Brook—then to be-
head and capture the stream itself. It now pours its waters through
the short gorge-like valley between Emerald and Margaree Forks to
join the stream that captured it.

Subsequent glacial action created Lake Ainslie, and the overflow of
this lake goes to swell the Margaree. Glacial debris choked the deserted river bed in the wind-gap, and formed the Lakes of Law.

The name *Margaree* is of Micmac origin, but of uncertain meaning.
French missionary priests almost invariably spell it *Magré*. Morris,
Crown-Land Surveyor, gives three variants, *Marguerite*, *Margaree*
and *Magré*, and applies the name to what is now Lake Ainslie.

9. Chéticamp is a land-tied island some six miles in length, lying parallel to the shore at a distance just short of half a mile. Three-
quarters of a mile from the island's southern tip (La Pointe), a gently
curving beach swings across to the mainland, forming a bay well sheltered from prevailing winds. At the time of Prenties' visit, this bay
was the only anchorage, since the mouth of the present harbour was
blocked by another beach. A channel was dredged in 1874, opening
the inner haven for vessels drawing up to twenty feet.

10. North from Cap Rouge, the massif that forms most of northern
Cape Breton drops precipitously to the water along a jagged shore. At
Pigeon Cove there is a slight embayment, where the tooth-like projec-
tions of sheer rock are more widely spaced than usual: Prenties' estimate of four hundred yards is not far out. Between these two projec-
tions, the sea has piled a beach of sand, gravel and cobblestones, that
changes in contour with every great storm from the westward. The
beach is backed by a sheer precipice varying in height between twenty
and forty feet, and from its top a sixty-degree slope rises more than a
thousand feet to the upland level. A wisp of a stream drops over the
precipice midway between the two projecting headlands, and loses itself in the rubble of the beach. In summer a swimmer could escape by
rounding either of the two headlands; if he were active and athletic he
could conceivably scale the precipice and follow up the slope. In winter conditions such as Prenties describes, escape would be impossible.

11. Fishing Cove is one and a half miles north of Pigeon Cove. Between the two lies the promontory known as White Capes, so called because a gigantic rockslide has scarred the precipice from top to bottom. From far at sea the scar stands white against the cliff.

At Fishing Cove the wall of rock was breached by a fault in ancient geological times. The waters of Fishing Cove River and its tributaries follow the fault-line to the ocean. Seen from out to sea, the cleft in the massif is spectacular. Perpendicular walls of rock form the entrance to a small cove, whose inner shore is a sandy beach. Before the advent of power-driven boats a small lobster factory was operated here by Robin & Jones, and two or three families (Frazers) had permanent homes. Today, only the bare fields, sloping to the stream, remain as evidence of human habitation. The old road to the cove meanders downward a good three miles from the top of MacKenzie Mountain.

Mr. Kenneth Timmons, of Pleasant Bay, was my boatman, guide and pleasant companion when I explored this coast.

12. Up to the landing in Pigeon Cove, Prenties' estimates of distances covered are surprisingly accurate. From Pigeon Cove on, his estimates are often badly off, even allowing for coastal contours. The actual straight-line distance from Pigeon Cove to Cape St. Lawrence is twenty-three miles; the sum of Prenties' estimated distances is exactly twice as great. Apparently the ice-laden boat moved more slowly through the water than its crew realized.

At Pleasant Bay, the massif recedes a little distance from the shore, and a shelf-like area of habitable land lies between the sea and the precipice. The wild valley of the Grand Anse opens on the southern end of the shelf, the valley of the Red River on the northern end. Beyond Red River the frowning massif marches again to the ocean shore, closing the vista.

13. That this landing was at Polletts Cove is made certain by the fact that here the castaways gave some thought to leaving the boat and striking inland. Between Pleasant Bay and Lowland Cove there is only one place where any thought of penetrating the massif could possibly be entertained: this is at Polletts Cove. (The name was originally *Poulet.*) Here, the two branches of the Blair River flow in a gentle valley and join their waters just before entering the ocean. But what seems at first glance to be an open way to the interior turns out to be a cul-de-sac. A mile from the shore, the rocky walls close in, the valley forks into smaller valleys that quickly narrow into canyons, where the waters leap down in falls and cataracts.

A family of MacGregors and one of Frasers were living at Polletts Cove in 1883; but the place has been long deserted. The old road, now a mere trail in much of its seven-mile length, runs from Red River Valley, high up above the shore; along it cattle are still driven to summer pasturage in the forsaken fields of the cove.

14. Sunrise Valley and its drowned extension, Aspy Bay, are dominated by the great escarpment of the Aspy Fault. Rising abruptly from the sea at Money Point, this straight, precipitous wall of rock, fourteen hundred feet in height, forms the northern shore of the bay and, striking inland for nearly twenty miles, "provides one of the most magnificent examples of shoreline scenery along the Atlantic coast." (D. W. Johnson: *The New England-Acadian Shoreline*, New York, 1925, p. 35.)

Part of the escarpment, but detached within it, where streams flowing in cross-faults have incised valleys, the Sugar Loaf rises to a peak, an outsize, displaced pyramid. From the shore below it, Aspy Beach extends in a four-and-a-half-mile crescent to Yellowhead, interrupted midway at Dingwall, where headlands push through to front the ocean. The beach cuts off behind it two large bodies of water, North Pond and South Pond, and two small narrow inlets, Dingwall Harbour and Middle Pond. All four of these are connected by channels with Aspy Bay.

Prenties and his companions landed at the end of the beach below the Sugar Loaf. Three miles out along the beach, at the mouth of Middle Pond, the ship *Auguste* drove ashore in 1761, with the loss of well over a hundred lives. Many of the victims were women, and for some years the beach was known locally as "Ladies Beach." St. Luc de La Corne was one of seven to come alive from the wreck.

(*1990 Editor's Note: Dr. Campbell was wrong about the location of the wreck of the Auguste. In July, 1977, divers Eddie Barrington and and Bob MacKinnon and their crews discovered the wreck in Dingwall Harbour—in 12 feet of water, about 1000 yards from shore.*)

15. Barrachois River and Indian Brook enter the ocean less than two miles apart. The detritus carried by these streams in their rapid descent from the uplands has built a common delta, straggling and irregular in shape, that trails off into the long beach that all but closes off St. Ann's Harbour. In some part of this low-lying area, the castaways made their last encampment.

16. "The amount of water retained in the body depends on the ratio of sodium ions to potassium ions in the blood. The more sodium, the

more water will be retained.... I can't think of anything more lethal than kelp to add to a diet of mutton fat for starving people. Its sodium content must be so high that any normal person who developed a fad for kelp would quickly find his legs swelling."—John Clegg, M.D.

17. Kelly's Mountain, sixteen miles in length, lies parallel to the face of the great northern upland, of which it is indeed a narrow, detached fragment. Enfolded between the two are St. Ann's Bay and its inner haven, St. Ann's Harbour. A three-mile beach slants across, almost joining one lofty precipitous shore to the other, and separates the bay from the harbour, except where the narrow channel allows the tides to ebb and flow.

Around the harbour are some low-lying areas, and the valleys of North River and other converging streams open vistas into the fastnesses of the interior. But never far away is the abrupt, stark face of the massif, in places falling sheer to the harbour, walling in the valleys, rising above field and forest, encompassing and enclosing the harbour and its arable.

18. Like Prenties, St. Luc de La Corne left a written account of his rescue by the Indians of St. Ann's. (*The complete narrative was published in English in* Cape Breton's Magazine, 18, 1977.) By collating his account with that of Prenties, and with local tradition, it is clear that the Indian encampment was located inland from the end of Goose Cove, five miles across the water from the harbour entrance. It was an advantageous location for a people who lived through the winter on caribou meat and seal oil. A short rapid climb brought the hunter to the high barren-lands where the caribou roamed, while the harbour itself was a common haunt of the seal.

Mr. John Erskine, whose work is opening new vistas in the prehistory of Nova Scotia, points out, in a letter to the writer, that the capture of Louisbourg and the removal from Cape Breton of its French inhabitants threw the Indian suddenly back on an old way of life. Liberal presents from the French king and traffic with French traders had in half a century done much to turn him from the old ways. Of necessity, the Indians who rescued first La Corne and then Prenties had gone back to the old staples of caribou meat and seal oil, and to their old winter hunting grounds. Within the memory of living men, a group of Indian families linked in matrilineal descent made the annual pilgrimage to St. Ann's. But they built their encampment on a beach near the end of Goose Cove, their old campsite having been preempted by the white man.

19. St. Luc de La Corne was no stranger to Ensign Prenties. After his

rescue by the Indians, St. Luc de La Corne returned overland to Quebec, making the trip in the depth of winter on snowshoes. One of the Canadian *noblesse*, he quickly became a figure of some importance in British Canada. In 1775 he was appointed to Quebec's first Legislative Council, and he was leader of the Indian detachment that accompanied Burgoyne on his ill-fated expedition. The Indians deserted Burgoyne before the final battle at Saratoga and St. Luc followed them back to Canada. He then visited England, where he made himself known to Lord George Germaine, Secretary of State for Colonial Affairs. Flamboyant in dress and manner, famous everywhere for his role in the old border wars, St. Luc was a familiar figure in Quebec and at the House of the Golden Dog. (For more concerning St. Luc, see Note 35.)

20. In strict truth, Prenties did not remain long with the Indians; he went as soon as he was able to an army outpost on Sydney Harbour. See the "Epilogue," beginning page 61.

21. Prenties returned to St. Ann's to pick up guides for the trip to Halifax. The first day's trek brought the party to the inlet of the Bras d'Or system known today as Big Harbour.

22. The second stage of their journey brought the travellers to the shores of Indian Bay; Prenties' distance of twelve and a half miles is about right. It is not surprising that Prenties found the geography of the lakes confusing; he would not see Lake St. Peter till after he crossed the portage at Estmere.

The name *Baddeck* was used by the Indians to designate Indian Bay and the area surrounding it. A shallow embayment opening into St. Patrick's Channel, this bay receives the waters of Baddeck and Middle Rivers. It seems to have had some special importance for the Micmac people. In 1766 Captain Samuel Holland's surveyors witnessed the great annual pilgrimage that brought hundreds of Indian families from mainland Nova Scotia to the shores of the bay.

It is a tribute to the strength and persistence of tribal custom that the Indian village of Nyanza is located today precisely where Holland found Indian "huts" two centuries ago. It must have been here that Prenties and his fellow travellers equipped themselves for passage along and through the lakes. (See Harvey, *op. cit.*)

23. Prenties' guides were taking him along a well-travelled route that led through Little Narrows and followed south along the shore to the short portage that gave access to the main body of the Bras d'Or complex, called Lake St. Peter by the French. Passing Estmere, the route

continued through the maze of islands and headlands that masks Denys Basin, and so came to Malagawatch.

Boom Island and Big Harbour Island, neither of which is an island, make up the strangely shaped peninsula, some five and a half miles in length, that the Indians called Malagawatch. Two-thirds of the peninsula is still mapped as an Indian reservation, and this for good reason. It was at Malagawatch that Father Gaulin established his mission to the Indians, even while the soldiers and engineers of France were laying the first foundations of Louisbourg. The location was astutely chosen, for it lay athwart the main route of Indian travel, and adjacent to Denys Basin where the best fishing in Cape Breton was to be found, and where the seal abounded. A church and presbytery were built at Malagawatch and, in succession, Fathers Gaulin, Courtain and Saint-Vincent carried on the work of the mission. They were followed by the famous Abbé Maillard who, in 1750, moved the mission to an island in St. Peters Inlet.

In 1744 Malagawatch was the scene of a poignant incident, memory of which has been all but lost in time's debris. Writing in 1755, Abbé Maillard recalled that, eleven years before, while he was visiting in Louisbourg, word came to him from Malagawatch that his Indians had taken five captive English children, tied them to trees, and killed them by using them for target practice. The good priest set off at once for his mission, there to vent the wrath of the church upon the murderers.

One can speculate that those nameless, hapless children, lost even to history, were taken prisoners in the early summer of 1744, when the Bras d'Or Indians joined Du Vivier's detachment from Louisbourg in a surprise attack on the English post at Canso. History records that the inhabitants of Canso were taken captive to Louisbourg, but the Indians must have spirited away a number of children to be sacrificed to the manes of fallen warriors.

(For the history of the Malagawatch mission, see the Reverend A. A. Johnston, *A History of the Catholic Church in Eastern Nova Scotia*, St. Fancis Xavier University Press, 1960. Abbé Maillard's letter dealing with the incident of the murdered children, is to be found in *Soirées Canadiennes*, 1863, p. 316.)

24. The Bras d'Or system is so complex that overall measurements are hard to come by. The distance from the entrance at Big Bras d'Or to the end of West Bay is fifty-three miles. Prenties is about right in his estimate of twenty miles for the widest part of Lake St. Peter. The shoreline of the lake is well over three hundred miles in length.

25. In open seasons the Indian traveller leaving Malagawatch pointed his canoe out into the lake, heading straight into the gullet of St. Peters Inlet. It is clear from Prenties' account that ice conditions forced his party to make the circuit of West Bay, before heading in St. Peters Inlet. Going the route he did, Prenties would see close to twenty islands—and many headlands that give the appearance of being islands.

26. Several early travellers have written of the generous hospitality accorded them in the Kavanagh establishment at St. Peters. It is uncertain whether the Kavanagh who entertained Prenties was Lawrence Kavanagh, Senior, or his son, also called Lawrence. Traboulsee states that the son, born in 1764, was seventeen years old when his father's death at sea left him in charge of the St. Peters establishment. It would appear that the father met his end some time in 1781.

Lawrence Kavanagh, Junior, is noted as the first Roman Catholic to take his seat in the House of Assembly in Halifax. (See A. A. Traboulsee, *Lawrence Kavanagh, His Life and Times*, Glace Bay, 1962.)

27. Grand Greve, an inlet of St. Peters Bay, is less than four miles from the village of St. Peters. To reach Isle Madame meant crossing a five-mile stretch of open water, which could be hazardous in a bark canoe if the waves were high. The travellers made the crossing the next day, reached the island at d'Escousse, and followed the shore around to Arichat.

28. The French knew the harbour of Arichat as *Porte Sainte Marie*, but the old Micmac name prevailed. Father Francois Lejamtel, writing in 1800, bears witness to the many changes in spelling the name has undergone.

"You ask me why I write Arischat while the people say Narischaque. When I arrived in this country, I saw all sorts of spellings applied to the place: Neireichak, Narichat, Anarichak, Anarowchack, Naurawchack, Narachaque, etc., etc., Arischat.... I think the reason for these different spellings is that it is an Indian name, whose pronunciation was not known distinctly, and everyone, whether English or French, wrote it as he thought proper...." (Quoted in Johnston, *op. cit.*)

29. Isle Madame is Madame Island on some recent maps. The main island and its covey of lesser islands were known to the French as *Iles de notre dame*, which may have derived from an older Portuguese name, *Ylas da Buena Madre* (W. F. Ganong, *Crucial Maps in the Early Cartography and Place Names of the Atlantic Coast of Canada*, University of Toronto Press, 1964). *Ile Madame*, a corruption of

the old French name, was current among the Acadians left in the area when other French populations had been removed from Cape Breton. As *Isle Madame*, pronounced in the English fashion, it found its place on nineteenth-century maps. The recent misfortune, Madame Island, is an inept anglicization that sacrifices euphony, buries tradition, defies local usage, and completes the transformation of an appellation of the Virgin Mary to a meaningless Madame. In the same fashion, *Ile Royale* has become the less melodious *Isle Royale*, but has thus far escaped the indignity of Royal Island.

30. In the early years of the Revolutionary War, American privateers knew well that they could find some who sympathized with the rebel cause in any Nova Scotian port they entered. Canso was notorious as a place into which and out of which the privateers could move with perfect freedom. It was due to Prenties' representations in London that a British cruiser was sent to Canso to put an end to the activities of the Americans.

NOTES TO THE EPILOGUE

31. Prenties' report is to be found in PAC, Haldimand Papers, Vol. 149, pp. 210-212.

32. A copy of this engraving, "The Departure," once the property of Senator J. S. MacLennan, now hangs in the James McConnell Memorial Library, Sydney. The engraving bears the following legend:

"THE DEPARTURE Of S. W. Prentice, Ensign of the 84th Regt & five others from their shipwrecked companions in the depth of winter 1781. Mr. Prentice was sent with public despatches from Gov. Haldimand at Quebec to Sir Heny Clinton at New York, who with 18 Seamen and Passengers, were cast away on a desolate uninhabited part of the Island of Cape Breton Dec. 5: 1780. Five perished and several lost their Fingers and Toes by the severity of the cold. The Survivors continued in this place several weeks when Mr. Prentice & such as were able embarked in a small Shattered Boat to seek some inhabited country. They stopped the leaks of their Boat by pouring Water on its Bottom till the holes were closed up with Ice. During a voyage of two months they suffered incredible hardships; at length worn out with fatigue, benumbed, diseased & famished. They were discovered by some of the Native Indians. These friendly Savages afterwards went to assist those who had been left at the Wreck of whom five only were found alive & they had subsisted many Days on the Bodies of their dead companions. See Ensign Prentice's Narrative.

"Painted by Robt Smirke. Engraved by Robt Pollard. London, Pubd March 8, 1784 by R. Pollard."

33. BM, *The London Review*, Vol. 67, 1782, p. 153.

34. BM, *The European Magazine*, Vol. 2, 1782, p. 132.

35. BM, *The Monthly Review*, Vol. 51, 1782, p. 481. This review concludes with an interesting reference to St. Luc de La Corne:

"The famous partizan—the closeted, confidential friend of Viscount Sackville, Mons. De Luc (*St. Luc de La Corne*), is introduced in this narrative; but without any credit to his honour or generosity. A poor Indian, who saved his life still regrets his failure in paying the promised reward. From a man who has kept company with '*honourable men*'—But we will say no more. He will be cited to a higher tribunal, where the claims of a poor Indian will not be despised."

There is a caustic gibe here that Londoners of the day would be quick to note—and relish. Viscount Sackville, better known as Lord George Germaine, was widely blamed for his conduct of the war in America and for its humiliating failure. In his youth Germaine had been court-martialed and cashiered for failing to obey orders on the battlefield of Minden, a failure that was attributed to sheer cowardice. The disgrace would have ruined a better man; but Germaine went on to become the confidant of George III, and the King's obedient instrument in his quest for personal rule. The quotation marks and the italics used in the review are an ingenious way of saying of the King's Minister what it might not have been wise to say more openly.

36. The findings of the court martial are in PAC, Haldimand Papers, Vol. B103, p. 395.

37. *The Proceedings of a Court of Inquiry* are in PAC, Haldimand Papers, Vol. 127, pp. 342-352.

38. PAC, Haldimand Papers, Vol. 213, pp. 205-215; see also Vol. 127, pp. 355-356.

39. PAC, Lower Canada Land Petitions, Vol. 160, 78494-5.

40. John Prenties served with Sir John Johnson's Corps, The King's Royal Regiment of New York.

41. Information concerning the Prenties brothers' activities in Gaspesia and Miramichi is contained in a memorial addressed to Governor Carleton of New Brunswick, and dated September 10, 1790. See also a counter-memorial by J. Black on behalf of William Forsyth & Com-

pany, dated November 18, 1790. (Department of Natural Resources, Fredericton, N. B.)

42. *The History of Miramichi* is a manuscript preserved in the New Brunswick Museum; Ganong attributes its authorship to Robert Cooney, author of *History of Northern New Brunswick*. One paragraph in the manuscript treats of the activities of the Prenties brothers on Bay du Vin Island. Oddly enough, the author names the two brothers as John and Thomas. I am indebted to the New Brunswick Museum for supplying me with a Xerox copy of the pertinent portion of the manuscript.

43. According to the War Office, London, Samuel Walter Prenties ceased to draw his retirement pay in 1799.

END of NOTES to Ensign Prenties' *Narrative*

ABOUT G. G. CAMPBELL

Born in Stewiacke, Nova Scotia, in 1904, and educated at
Dalhousie University, Dr. George Graham Campbell came
to Cape Breton as Principal of Sydney Academy, serving
from 1935 till his retirement in 1968. He earned a reputa-
tion as a consummate educator, particularly in history, ge-
ology, mathematics, Latin and Greek. He fought for imple-
mentation of business education, and he challenged com-
munity norms in promoting quality educational facilities
for all people, regardless of religious affiliation. In 1950, he
was Canadian representative at the UNESCO Seminar in
Brussels, and he received an honorary doctorate from St.
Francis Xavier University. Dr. Campbell is the author of
History of Nova Scotia. He died in 1972, and he is buried
adjacent to the farm where he was born.